APACHE

APACHE

WILL LEVINGTON COMFORT

University of Nebraska Press
Lincoln and London

Copyright 1931 by E. P. Dutton & Co., Inc.
All rights reserved
Manufactured in the United States of America

First Bison Book printing: 1986
Most recent printing indicated by the first digit below:
1   2   3   4   5   6   7   8   9   10

Library of Congress Cataloging-in-Publication Data
Comfort, Will Levington, 1878–1932.
  Apache.
  "Bison."
  1. Mangas Coloradas, Apache chief, d. 1863?—
Fiction. 2. Apache Indians—Fiction.
I. Title. [PS3505.042A84 1986]   813'.4   85-29021
ISBN 0-8032-6319-8 (pbk.)

Reprinted by arrangement with E. P. Dutton,
a division of New American Library

FOREWORD

About seven years before the year 1800, an Apache later known as Mangus Colorado was born near the old Copper Mines on the Mimbres River in what is now Grant County, southwestern New Mexico. To the north are the Pinos Altos mountains and the Mogollons, also the headwaters of the Gila, which the Indians speak of as the river that flows into the sunset without end.

The exact time of Mangus Colorado's birth is not known, but in 1863 he was said to be seventy years old, and at that time the most celebrated physically and mentally, the rim-rock Apache, of his race. "The King Philip of the Apache nation," wrote Captain Cremony in 1868. "Beyond all comparison the most famous Apache warrior and statesman of the century."

Of his early years little is known; he merely ran with the herd. He was late in making his warrior name, and was spoken of familiarly as Dasoda-hae (He that is just sitting there) from his propensity to stay awake listening to the words of his elders, hours after others of his age had crawled in. Camp wear and tear abbreviated this to Don-Ha which he carried until the time came for him to compel his chosen identification—Mangus Colorado (Red Sleeve)—which came to be spoken by all men between the Rio Grande and the Colorado, a name that lives, because born of thoughts carried out.

5

Back of Mangus Colorado was said to be Maco, a big chief of the Mimbreno Apaches, of whom nothing is known except by the word of Geronimo, who was a man of many words which mainly ran together in himself. Geronimo said that Maco was his grandfather, and that Mangus Colorado was a lieutenant of Maco, when he— the greatest of Apache talkers—was just a little boy.

Before the coming of white frontiersmen, all foreign association of the Apaches was with the Nakai-yes (Mexicans) from whom they received their Spanish names. The Apaches were secretly proud of these names. More often than not they were blood-bought.

Soldado Fiero and Juan Jose were active chiefs at the time Mangus Colorado was growing up. The first was a great raider, but not wise in counsel. Juan Jose seems not to have been outstanding in either branch. Had he not proved weak enough to permit the Mexicans to resume work at the Copper Mines in 1804, many pages of southwestern history would not have been written; others would have read far differently. However, Juan Jose stepped one day from the side-lines into the very center of the picture for one unfading print, after which he stepped no more. His passing marked the assumption of Mangus Colorado's leadership.

apache

apache

I

Two DAYS' sun to the east of the Copper Mines was the Big River. Don-Ha's people were attracted that way in large numbers in the spring months to renew their acquaintance with other than drinking water. Camp smoke and body grime were well enough in the cold season, but became rancid when the sun was well turned northward. Heads of small children and most of the adults were infested by this time with life that became aggressive in the balmy air.

Rio Grande mud was great medicine for this. The squaws covered the heads of the young ones in a thick pack of mud, making them sit still in the sun until the cast cracked. It was interesting to see the denizens caught for keeps in the inside of the broken pieces of the mud cap.

The Apache is not a fish eater, but there were feasts of duck and brant. It was boy business to get these—no wasting of arrows, either. In the river bottoms grew a big gourd. The pith was not good to eat, but the shells made handy vessels. When the birds were on the river, the boys strung the gourds together and let them float down stream among the favorite feeding-places of the waterfowl. At first the birds were restless and took wing, but after a few days, they became used to the queer bobbing, and in due time paid no attention. Nor did they later notice the slight alteration in the gourds, peek-holes and the like, nor the boys beneath them with bags weighted with stones, pulling the birds under from time to time.

Don-Ha did not get much chance at this; gourds rarely grew big enough for that head. But he could swim all day, and lengthening out as he was, much swimming took up the slack. Lost Pony, one of his companions, was good at this silent duck hunting, and another companion called Black Knife, the son of Soldado Fiero, was exceptional in all matters of the kind. At reading trail and at antelope stalking, Black Knife had no rival for his age. On all fours, covered in deerskin with head and antlers attached, he had actually been shot at from the far side of a grazing herd. This was a real honor. Antelope was no fool like waterfowl. You couldn't get among them in their own dress, but with a lot of practice and patience one could get close, and have time to sink three or four arrows, before the herd was off for the day.

Another way of stalking antelope for a set of shots was for one boy to skirt the herd at a distance, keeping under cover, all except a long lance with a fluttering pennon on top. The deer became absorbed to drooling over this, but kept their distance. It was far more easy than usual at such times for others to stalk within range from the opposite side.

On the way between the Copper Mines and the Rio Grande was the hill of the hot springs—Ojo Caliente, it was later called by the Mexicans. Older people of the tribe thought highly of coming here to boil out after the chill had left the air. The squaws had to be driven off, they liked it so well. This was a place of conference also; head men and medicine men sitting for hours waiting for those thoughts which come best when the sweat is flowing freely. Don-Ha would sit in the steam as long as he was permitted to remain.

In the high country to the north there was big timber and springs and waterfalls where the heat of midsummer was tempered, and there was much tanning and venison-jerking to be done and baskets to weave. While squaws managed these affairs, the men hunted, leaving the bears alone, since the Apache has a truce with the bear. Some-times the boys were allowed to go along; but mainly they went on excursions by themselves.

In the time of great heat, there was Spinning Falls to go to. Its uppermost cup was far up on the mountain-side. Here the water bounced into a huge smooth basin and one could sit in the spray until chilled to the bone and then step out onto a dry cleft and know what it meant to be brought back to life by the sun on the rocks.

Boys looked into bear business for clues to the honey hives. This was the main store of sweet, and greatly desired for pinole which is a flour made of mesquite beans and acorns. To come into camp with deer sacks heavy with crushed comb—eyes flamed from the smudges, bodies welted with stings and stomachs loathly sick from the incidental debauch—was a real way to acquire merit. Then along the smaller streams were the arrow canes and lance wood, and mulberry branches for bows, and stones already rounded for metates. Much time was spent in the manufacturing of all these. The squall of a wildcat put them on duty at once. The best possible quiver of arrows was made of the wildcat's pelt, with the tail hanging down.

To the west of the Copper Mines was one of the chief

treasures of the Mimbrenos, one of the best proofs of their stand-in with Usen, the Creator. This was the incomparable grazing lands which kept the horses pinked-up like grain. No forage anywhere like grama grass. Another band of Apaches lodged in the Chihuicahui* mountains, grazed their animals on it from the west, but were not nearly so well off in other ways.

Don-Ha often overheard the warriors discussing the habitats of the other wings of the tribe—the Mescaleros east of the Big River where the land flattened out and became all alike and the water was unfit to drink; the Coyoteros to the northwest where the dust rose like smoke around them when they travelled; the Navajos who sat freezing in snow and ice half the year and spent the other half weaving blankets to live through until spinning time again. The Jicarillos and their country were similarly discussed; the Tontos and Pinals, and others, not Apache, with more consuming scorn. There is no derision like that of the Mimbreno Apache, when he speaks the words "farmer" or "sheep-herder," and these words were connected variously with the Pimas, Navajos, Maricopas, Yumas and Opatas. By all means the Mimbrenos were well off. The country of the Copper Mines had been the stronghold of their fathers. There was none like it elsewhere.

---

*Chiricahua.

II

D ON-HA was not given particularly to boy friendships, being a listener of elders always, but there was Lost Pony, the son of a highly respected tribesman, and Black Knife, whose father, Soldado Fiero, was a chief, second only to Juan Jose in the counsels of the tribe. With these two, Don-Ha's education was conducted one summer under the tutelage of a lame Apache, a younger brother of Soldado Fiero, called Kaiben-digo, Foot and a Half, or Half-Foot, whose prowess was all in the head.

Half-Foot was in the medicine lodge much of the time working with sickness and advice to others, with old Ne-pot-on-je, the Bear Watcher, and Wano-boono, Calico Turkey. He had been spoiled as a boy by a falling horse. His heel was drawn up and stiffened so that only the forward part of the imprint of his right foot showed. He was very ugly, like the whole Soldado Fiero household, but an Apache in every link of the spine.

There were great lessons in stealth and background identification and motionless sitting.

Rise-from-the-grass—is synonym for Apache in his own concept. To rise from the grass was a prevailing art; to surprise another within three or four feet, a form of play from babyhood. The one surprised or taken off his guard is in disgrace. The quail is past master in this profession and to the Apache one of the most approved forms of bird life. It is not only a matter of sitting still, but of thinking still, of emptying the mind. If you do not wish your adversary to know your plan, you must not even think it when he is near until the instant of coup. This is a far deeper fold of the game than a mere motionless huddling against a rock. It has to do with the science of invisibility mentioned in high medicine lore.

Frequently Don-Ha with other Apache youths was taken to the pasture lands and ordered to hunt cover at signal. The neatness and dispatch of the competitors were judged by experts. Again they were released by signal to plant themselves among the boulders or yucca butts—or vanish into any cover or background the land held. They used gray blankets at times or covered themselves with dirt.

Rise-from-the-grass. Tloh-ka-dih-nadidah-hae.

Many trips that summer with the limping one for teacher and guide. He was never a friend. Like all Apaches, the three boys were taught from the very beginning how not to get lost. Nothing brings down the ninny-cry upon a boy's head so quickly as to lose his way. They were taken out moonless nights and released to find camp. In coming to a strange ridge, they were told to stop and study it from a distance; then from halfway, finally from close-up. It was literally photographed on the brain. There were warriors among the Mimbrenos who could not be lost in all the land between the Rio Grande and the Colorado and who could find practically all the springs and water holes in the vast terrain.

One day five miles from the Copper Mines, Half-Foot and the three boys came upon cougar-tracks. This is another master at hiding himself in the scenery.

"When he go by here?" Half-Foot asked.

"Last night." This was granted.

"Where he sit now?"

Don-Ha pointed to the thick green strip low in the distance. It was far ahead, but water was there and Half-Foot led the way. Either he granted that Don-Ha was right or was taking pains to show him up. It was well known that the cougar, though not liking water more than any other cat, appreciates the big trees only found near water, except in high country. Dense shade at midday for the cougar family.

Whatever Half-Foot saw, he made no effort to find tracks on the way. They cut straight for the river bank where the cougar prints were seen again. Now they silently traced these to a large tree. One thing to find a cougar tree; quite another to find himself or herself up in the dark of the leaves, stretched out still as the limb itself, head cocked to one side and squinting so his eyes would not shine out and betray. You didn't really see a cougar after all; you somehow became aware of him in the mind at last and then his outer silhouette appeared. A minute afterward you wondered how your eyes could have missed so long. Black Knife was a devil for finding the cougar on the branch. It was he who gave the first sign. Half-Foot may have seen before this, or may not. Anyway he said nothing until the beast was pointed out.

"Cougar run and hide all day from Indian, but when he sees death he no more run. Cougar slow die, no fear; take Indian boy with him to die too; take two boys if he can. Shoot straight, so he come down all in heap, no longer see—"

This was straight Apache philosophy and readily understood. The Apache himself keeps death from his body as long as possible; there are no suicides, but when the end is unescapable from mortal wound, there is nothing to lose and no fear in the world. The fighting death is then the thing.

So the three considered carefully and released their arrows together. Down came the squalling, sprawling cat, not done-for, but three arrows in his chest, and nothing left but his own swift-striking paralysis to fight. Half-Foot showed them which arrow had done best and why. It was Don-Ha's, and he was awarded the pelt.

III

Boys and horses. Boys from ten to seventeen did most of the tribal herding. They were never apart from horses. To be without the smell of horses would mean not only that they had not ridden, but that they had not eaten. Apacheria was south of bison ranges; they had no sheep save as novelty from occasional forages among the Navajos. They raised no grain or fruits or cattle. Wild horses did not come to them. The few ranges of incomparable grama grass were walled off by vast waterless tracts of thorn and rock. Spring was the time for replenishing raids therefore, not only for mounts, but for food stock.

Boys were not taught to ride. There were no horses too bad to try out, too vicious not to be contained in the combined knowledge of a group. The reata was an inspired extension of their thin arms; the beast itself an auxiliary of narrow knees. What they lacked in strength they accomplished in agility. What one did not think of in the way of ingenious deviltry, the group mind spawned. In a herd of a hundred fresh ponies, there were no secrets of speed or stamina unfathomed in a week. With their backs turned they could designate any animal, a gesture and a guttural. Anatomy was an open book. In the case of a bad fall, it was mainly the horse that broke himself; the boys came to the ground standing. Once useless, the horse was on the grill while still hot and his hide staked out. Nor was his blood spilled on the ground, nor his viscera left to the birds.

They ran horses, broke them until the beasts had no will, but only a sweating horror at their approach. Half-Foot showed them how to make a horse kill himself; how to make him do an added mile at top speed, after he is ready to quit. He diagrammed the best cuts of meat; the quickest cuts to take from a fallen horse when time presses on the warpath. He initiated them in the endless craft of stealing horses; how to study a herd to ascertain the leader, how to hold the rest together through him single-handed. One of their great games was stealing horses from each other; all the ways of doing this were closely inquired into and practised in preparation for work on corrals of the Nakai-yes (Mexicans) later.

Half-Foot told the story of a great coup his brother Soldado Fiero had pulled off when he was making a name for himself. There was a Mexican corral full of valuable horses, but kept under lock and special night guard. That corral was a veritable stockade, no chance of breaking in; the posts parted the best of rope saws. Soldado Fiero, then a young brave without lasting name, climbed the wall in the night and hid among the horses until daybreak. A dozen vaqueros stood outside ready to reata their mounts when the big gates were opened, and Soldado, clinging to the side of the leader of the herd, straightened up the instant he passed forth into the open and gave a series of whoops that made the horses forget breakfast and all else until they were twenty miles away in the hands of Apache herders. He had run off the whole corral-full single handed by conquering the will of the king horse. Such matters were not readily forgotten.

IV

EARLY one morning Don-Ha, Lost Pony and Black Knife had no sooner sat up than they were blindfolded. This did not disturb them; they knew it to be an incident of training. Half-Foot led them out of camp and finally gave the word for them to uncover their heads.

They were moving out toward the grass lands and presently struck a man-party trail. In dry season, grass that has been trampled does not "come back," but gradually toasts down, finally to dust. Half-Foot paused over a small bedded patch aside from the trail they were on, and told them to read what they could.

The boys pressed about, careful not to disturb the body mold. It was too small for a cow or pony. There was positively no detectable odor. The three heads bent long and low. Delicately at last Black Knife's hand moved among the grass stems and picked out a small matted tuft of brown fur. This he smelled with fine discrimination.

"Huh—how you know that?" asked Half-Foot.

"Feel—smell—see. This is because he scratched."

"When did he make bed here?"

They tested the withered stems and compared the fresher stems of the standing grass. Three decisions were imparted privately to Half-Foot, each to the effect that the dog had lain on this spot two days ago.

The trail was continued. They had been blindfolded, so they could have no means of knowing the nature of the party and if it were still out from camp. This was a day's work; they followed for miles and hours, frequently pausing for close examination. It was a trick trail. A great variety of signs were there—bent twigs—broken sticks—misplaced stones. It passed over grass land, gravel beds and through mesquite screens. It crossed other trails and an arroyo with water in the bottom. It circled back to camp and then opened up, the members of the party taking different directions to their teepees. It was late in the afternoon when the boys reached the place where they had taken their blinders off in the morning. They had not yet broken their fast.

Don-Ha's head and senses had been in intense occupation for many hours. He reported eight people in the party—three braves, three squaws; one boy with moccasin on one foot and Mexican boot on the other; one little one barefoot, either boy or girl. Also three ponies and two dogs. One of the ponies was a mare. The trail was made yesterday afternoon and evening; at least, the party did not reach the arroyo until afternoon. Party made sign of being gone three days, but did not carry out the word. Two squaws kneeled to drink at edge of water. Cattle trail crossed Apache trail on the far bank of the arroyo— five or six cattle from Mimbreno range. Antelope trail crossed at bend-back of Indian party toward Copper Mines. Antelope trail cold—two—three days. Party left sign of going deeper into grass lands, but did not carry out sign. Left sign of being in need of aid and for supports to follow, but returned instead. Left sign of bad news and again that expedition was successful—

Don-Ha's report was not considered full nor in the least extraordinary. It was no better than Lost Pony's and not so good as Black Knife's, who had discerned that there were but seven Mimbrenos in the party and not eight; two squaws instead of three. He accounted for this by saying that the boy had gone barefoot part of the way, while the smaller squaw had put on the Mexican boot. Even Black Knife did not know whether the littlest foot was that of boy or girl, but he was more explicit about the game-trail. This was his specialty, as it was the specialty of Soldado Fiero, his father, who had brought these readings to a point of sorcery.

Black Knife was right about there being seven in the party instead of eight. All three had faultlessly deduced the presence of the dogs and ponies, also that one of the latter was a mare. The way she had stood in certain functioning proved that.

The trail showed best at the arroyo. It was here that the boys determined beyond doubt that the party passed there yesterday, and in the afternoon, because the displacement had not dried enough to show the effect of a full day's sun, or even exposure to mid-day sun of one day. It was here also that the squaws were finally isolated. Knee marks were visible where they bent to drink. The male Apache rarely kneels to drink. He places his hands in the water, so as to leave no sign but the tips of his moccasins, and often blurs these. His knees are also narrower. The narrow sharp heel of one cast-off Mexican boot alternately worn by the boy and a smaller squaw was the feature of the day. Black Knife gained merit in working that out. He was making a name for himself literally.

The other messages were matter of exact knowledge.

Stones have their weathered side and earthy side. They naturally fall heavy-side-down or settle to that position in heavy rains. A disturbed stone is at once a lithograph. Out of place it is as obvious as a misplaced letter on a printed page. Overturned, it signifies indifferent success of an expedition; partly turned over, bad news, disaster. A stone on end leaning against another is a call for aid. A line of stones heavy side down, as naturally, reports success—these but a few details of the code.

Animal manure is one of the chief points studied in determining the nature of that which has made the trail. Its degree of dryness is one of the best tests of the time elapsed since the transit. By its composition the direction a party has come from is determined, because of the Apache's marvelous knowledge of his habitat. Bunch grass, bear grass, buffalo grass, all tell of districts. Don-Ha knew the cattle belonged to the Mimbreno range because the trail showed the waste of grama grass alone. Corn would have told of a Mexican party.

Don-Ha was not disturbed upon being informed that Black Knife excelled him in this critical day's work. Black Knife was always reading, following, losing himself in the writing of men and animals. Don-Ha was given to thinking about other things. He was the listener; he put two and two together. He could forget himself in his own thoughts as Black Knife forgot himself in signs on the ground. His time was not yet.

V

O NE DAY when the main body of the Mimbrenos was at the Big River, couriers reached them from those behind at the Copper Mines with word that a big party of Spaniards and Nakai-yes had come up from Chihuahua prepared to stay. Also others were coming. Don-Ha stood near Soldado Fiero when the message was delivered. The Apache leader had the look of one snake-bitten. Juan Jose was back in camp, and had evidently not driven the interlopers away at their first appearance.

Don-Ha felt weighty affairs impending. Over all was a mighty curiosity to see the strangers. He had seen Nakai-yes, but never one of the pale Spaniards, the holders of great lands and authority in the country below. Black Knife was at hand, with the same look of his father. This meant war to Don-Ha's idea, and life now took on its essential meaning.

Juan Jose was found to be dealing with the strangers. He had taken their presents. His eyes were wildly bright with their firewater like one who had come into sudden sense of his own unparalleled importance, with un-dreamed of riches at his disposal. He explained that the Spaniards wanted nothing but "cobre"; that they had no intention of over-running the country but merely to pack "cobre" from the mountains and send it back to their country with mules; that the mules coming back from their country would bring many presents for the Indians —blankets, maize, beads, ornaments of white iron, knives, wines, coffee. Later, pesh-e-gar, the rifle, would be placed

23

in Apache hands, making the Mimbreno indisputably superior to all people. The Spaniards would establish their "cobre" camp in one place and keep to it; also they would travel with their mule trains over one route only into the southeast, and one other into the southwest.

"The Mimbreno will still be lord of his land," Juan Jose said, "and these people will bring in everything desired—"

There were many who agreed with him, and others who resented intrusion in any form, at any price. There were older Mimbrenos, Ne-pot-on-je and Wano-boono chief among them, who hinted that these things all had been tried before; that Spaniards had come and nothing was the same afterward, the integration of the Mimbrenos broken; that it had become necessary to drive out the Spaniards with great loss of braves. Many of the younger Indians wanted the change; and these stayed with Juan Jose at the old camp in the Copper Mines; others preferred privacy and the older order, and these established a base at the Warm Springs eastward under Soldado Fiero. Don-Ha's people were among those who stayed.

All these things happened gradually. There would be weeks, even months, of waiting for a single train, which the Spaniards called their "conductas." A garrison of Mexican soldiers was established at Janos, several days' sun to the south. The mining camp itself became a Mexican village—Santa Rita del Cobre—an outpost of Janos, with senoritas, stores, miners' families coming in and making their buildings of clay. A big three-cornered presidio was also built. The Mimbreno stronghold at the Copper Mines became no stronghold at all.

Finally a Spanish priest came and a little mission was

built for him in Santa Rita. He did not stay there, for it was said he was also the Medicine Padre of the old stone church in Janos, and this was merely to be one of his visitas. When he came to Santa Rita del Cobre, however, it did not suffice for him to remain among the miners in the village. Very soon he climbed to the Mimbreno camp to tarry there, and even turned his mule one day toward the inner camp of Soldado Fiero, making his signs and talking of peace. His purpose, he said, was to cement friendship and understanding between two kinds of men, who were the same, not one above the other, in the sight of God.

No Mexican would have gone alone to the inner camp. Don-Ha followed at a distance. The white Medicine Padre was unafraid. He saw no need apparently to protect himself. He said he was protected. He was not afraid of sickness, which all Mimbrenos shunned. Don-Ha followed and listened to his talk. He knew how ugly Soldado Fiero's people were. Always the Padre talked. It seemed to matter little to him that no Mimbrenos knew what he said. He had dealings with the sky and the sun. He shortened himself to his knees on the ground, which no Mimbreno would do if he were afraid. He raised his arms to the sky with shut eyes and issuing talk. The Mexicans took off their hats when he came near, and bobbed their heads, keeping their faces to him. Big Medicine, past doubt. The Mimbreno medicine men resented all this. Old Ne-pot-on-je talked long against it and Wano-boono egged him on.

These two were highly held by all Mimbrenos. Don-Ha did much of his listening by the fire of their medicine lodge. Ne-pot-on-je chose wisdom as a youth, rather than war, and went to the bear to get it. His name signified as much, Bear Watcher. The squaws said that it was not the bear, but Wano-boono (Calico Turkey) that was the source of Ne-pot-on-je's wisdom, but braves do not listen to squaws. Though not man and wife, these two hunted in couple about their devious medicine affairs. They were not so inclined to send Dor-Ha about his business, as other medicine people, and too well established to live in the fear of being spied upon. Indeed they predicted that Don-Ha would end up in the deeps of sorcery and stand behind the throne of his people, rather than in the center of it, the latter requiring little wisdom.

Don-Ha never wearied of looking at Calico Turkey. As a little girl, she had been mauled and mangled by a mountain lion, the skin of her face and arms was seamed and streaked as if put back hurriedly. Also she had once been captive in a Nakai-yi village far to the south, and while there had contracted that sickness which leaves deep pits upon the flesh. Yet she could whirl like a leaf and spring to her feet from flat sitting and dance until the eyeballs of all others who tried to keep up were on the point of bursting from their sockets. Also she talked the language of the Nakai-yes long before the miners came to Santa Rita del Cobre.

VI

O F ALL Apaches who listened to the words of Father
Font, one with great head, long arms and saddle-bowed
legs came most often and was most apt to stay after
others were gone. The priest learned Apache at first
much faster than Don-Ha learned Spanish, but this was
not so afterward when the young Mimbreno set his mind
to task.

One thing which Don-Ha gradually learned in his
visits to Santa Rita was the value of money. No Apache
ever learned this before to the same degree. Hunger
taught him. His great thick trunk of a body had always
hunger in it like a young hound. His tastes taught him,
for he had learned to like many things to eat and drink—
chili dishes, tortillas, vinos, coffee. Waiting was one
means to get these things—sitting around looking at the
places where they were. Dogs know this way. They sit
and watch a door when the smells are coming out, but
it is a hard and slow way.

Begging was a way, but it was harder still. There was
that in the Apache which made it easier for him to turn
his back when things were being passed than to hold out
his hand as Mexican beggars did. A fierce, swift stiffening of pride that put out the hunger for a time as water
puts out fire.

Stealing was a way—the old good way, but the Mexicans let one know that they knew the next time one came,
and besides the Medicine Padre was averse to stealing,
talked much against it.

Another way was to bring into Santa Rita skins, baskets, mesquite beans, wild honey, horses, cattle, and trade these for the things in the village. But it was slow work and much had to be given for little to those who sat in their shops and had nothing else to do but make trade from morning until night. Besides, when one brought in horses or cattle many questions were asked; it was really simpler to eat the meat of the animals than to carry it a great distance.

There was still another way. This was to work in the village with the tools of the Mexicans—to hoe and dig holes, but two or three hours of this would not do. One was supposed to do it all day and again the next day, and this brought upon one the silence of the men of his own people and the laughter of the squaws.

Still money was a powerful thing; a little of it always surprised Don-Ha at what it could do. A circle of it in the palm of the hand was as heavy as the hindquarters of a mule. But money took much thinking to get, and all the ways of getting it had to be gone over again and again to be understood. Don-Ha tried all these ways, and thought of them all, one after another, from which it is to be seen that there was hunger in his head as well as in his belly.

Stealing was simplest and best, but the Medicine Padre did not like that.

There were reasons why Don-Ha continued to listen. He learned to speak the language; he learned the life of the village; he was fed for listening, and though he became at times very tired in the head, two or three weeks later at most he wanted to go back. Much of the Padre's talk was worthless, but some of it was the talk of men.

To hear that one had to hear other things, for instance, of one born of a virgin—

Nothing to stir an Apache in that. The Mimbreno tradition ran somewhat the same—of a virgin who had every reason for being wanted by men, but who would take none of them. Alone in the sun and alone in the night was her idea. And one day at the time of a great drouth she was lying on a rock when a drop of dew fell upon her, and she had a son, unlike any other son, who made himself listened to for many years and whose mistakes were never found out.

The son of the Padre's virgin, on the contrary, was found out. Moreover, he was not great enough to save himself from being tortured on a cross. A cross was familiar. Don-Ha could put two and two together. A cross and the sahuara were not unlike. Torture and the giant cactus were always with one. Besides, that which the Padre talked of happened very long ago.

But as a price for hearing what one wanted to hear, one listened to all the Padre had to say. Always the price to pay, but other things were good. Through the years, matters like these began to be familiar:

"Listen, Don-Ha. You are to be a good Indian, and have power for good among your people. You are to be a bridge between your people and my people. This, you must learn first—that we are not all the same. If one of us does wrong, do not blame us all. And this remember always—that I will not change toward you or your people—that I am here to be one thing to you—to stand when others change and keep your faith. If one man breaks faith with you, do not blame us all. Wait till I break faith with you."

This was patiently and powerfully impressed. It was a part of the day's labor in the fold. It would appear that Father Font already recognized in Don-Ha an outstanding Apache and was building protection for his own people later by establishing a bond between the village and this "future great"; yet the Padre was doubtless capable of building in a principle for its own sake. Perhaps he also knew that this could only be done in the case of an Apache in the transition period of boyhood, before the tribal fixation of character settled. But even he did not know how set and persistent was the racial inheritance of the Apache breed, nor how it "threw back" in the man, in spite of boyhood innovations.

Don-Ha's head was getting even bigger. He was living up to his name of just sitting there, but much that the Padre said was merely words:

"Listen, Don-Ha—there is a light! I have seen that light. It is not a shaded light that shines one way. It is like a fire in an open place sending its light all ways. No wind can blow out that light; no water can wet it. And this is the nature of that light—that looking out from it, one can see all ways—into days not come as well as days that are lived, into things undone as well as those accomplished, into the future as well as the past—"

All of which was part of the price to be paid. Anyone knew there were winds and rains that put out fires—any fires; that looking out of the firelight one could see little or nothing in any direction, but that looking from the dark one could see far and truly. But always after much squaw talk came moments of man talk:

". . . and in that light, I see great wanderings, great distances, terrible hunts of men, the scorpion on the ground, the eagle gone from the air . . . and you, Don-Ha, with arm raised in the midst of many tribes—an arm red with blood to the elbow—"

That was good. It stirred heatedly among the inert masses of tissue in the great dim head. It was the inception of his name, no less. The rest did not stand up with it, did not portend so much:

"But this need not be, Don-Ha. It is but one side and you may choose the other. It need not be, if you remember you are a bridge; a bridge between two people that they may become brothers. It need not be, if you remember that some of us are good, some are evil; that we are not all one. Choose the good, be true to the good. Oh, be faithful, my son, and may God help me to be faithful to you to the end—help me to see it in times of darkness, as I see it now in that light."

Because the Padre impressed upon him many times the thought of the bridge, Don-Ha came to ponder upon it alone. The thought was not acceptable.

"A bridge—" he grunted, staring into the fire, "a bridge to walk on—huh—no walk on me!"

A rock standing high in the land was far more to his liking than a bridge. And the red arm raised above many tribes—that was acceptable.

Words meant little or nothing of themselves, except when they mounted to picture-making power, but years of words began to mean something, and years of consistent friendship on the part of the Medicine Padre meant much. There were times when Juan Jose "went bad" even to Santa Rita, and drove off horses and cattle from the corrals surrounding the town; times when the Mexicans in turn would have called out the soldiers from the sleepy barracks at Janos, to run out the Apaches from the Mines except for the intervention of the priest. Once Don-Ha heard him tell his own people, the Nakai-yes:

"The Indians are but children, if we can be fathers. Be patient—do not strike or be angry. They will come and go and bring equivalent for that which they take. But if we cannot be good fathers—they cannot be other than devil's children."

And that is why Juan Jose, fresh from depredations elsewhere, stalked into the Copper camp of Santa Rita and grunted his wish for mescal, tobaho and cafe.

VII

Don-Ha was the tallest man in Juan Jose's wing of the Mimbrenos, and still growing. One day while stalking antelope, a doe first to sense alarm, hopped out of the feeding circle, and fell with an arrow on either side. One was from Lost Pony, the other from Don-Ha's bow. This they took for a sign of fellowship. As they rode in with strips of venison hanging from their saddles, Lost Pony imparted the information that his sister Parah-dee-ah-tran was just about ready to take a husband; that the news presently would be circulated. Private information like this was as clean-grained evidence of respect as one young man could show another. Don-Ha accepted the tribute and said he would think it over.

This he did. The more he thought the more the idea of taking the girl grew and drove other thoughts from his mind. Before now he had looked upon Lost Pony's sister, but without opening to her in sudden infatuation as the Apaches recognize it. He realized that she had been put into his head by her brother. Still the result was much the same.

The name Parah-dee-ah-tran means one without cares in this world, of contented disposition. The single word "Placid" expresses it as well as any. Don-Ha had wrestled with her sometime before—a boy and girl tussle in the evening when the young Apaches were at play like animals. It was just a moment. She was cool and weak, her laughter unturbulent. She slid out of his hands. He would have forgotten it entirely had not Lost Pony spoken this thing.

Placid's readiness was announced. Don-Ha went over to her father's teepee and sat with other young men in the evening. This diminished and angered him. He did not feel that he should go into the running with other swains. He hardly saw Placid that night. She was in her high hour; she had come into her light. She had her bells on; also tinsel, beads, bracelets. They were beating the oxhide for her behind the teepee. She commanded the situation—her parents like shadows merely in their own lodge. She was supposed not to know her own mind. She looked no boy in the face; she laughed and moved among them. Don-Ha drank tizwin and grew uglier.

That was the night of the ninya (virgin) dance in Placid's honor. Many Mimbreno girls attended her. Old Calico Turkey put on the tribal robe of beaded buckskin with paintings of bright red and blue dye upon it. There were also faded symbols of dark red made from the dried blood of a beef-heart. Around a big fire, the girls gathered in a hollow square with Placid in the center. They closed upon her with a weird sing-song chant; then drew back and shaded their eyes with their hands looking into the night-sky for lovers of their own; they closed in upon her again, breathed and sung with their lips close to Placid's body, until she was folded within folds of her kind, and all the watching braves were excited.

Then old Calico Turkey sang alone. In the height of her song she plucked a brand from the fire and thrust it into Placid's hand. It was Placid's work then to keep this alive as long as possible, but it did not prosper in her languid handling. It burned a little, but the flames were outward bound. It flickered and went dark at half-way. All heads nodded then and a murmur was heard above the crackling of the fire. Placid's life-line as thus read was brief.

Don-Ha left at last. It happened just then that Placid was apart from the others. She touched his hand, put something in it; no object. Her hand was cool, glidy, narrow; it lay open against his palm; afterward it was as if it were still there. It lasted like a bee-sting.

VIII

H<small>IS</small> GOING to her lodge announced a casual interest merely. Nothing need come of it, unless he wished. Yet he did wish something to come of it. He was not himself; he was drawn as if by the girls' hand leading his thoughts. There were two ways to break this; one by taking her, the other by turning his back upon her and heading out on a long hunting raid.

He chose the easier. Several afternoons later he led his best pony down to the water and swam it about in a deep hole until it was clean. Then he plucked burrs from the matted tail one by one; after that he fed the beast to a fullness rarely known in the treatment of Apache animals. It was now dark, a soft early moonless dark, and Don-Ha saddled and rode to the water, permitting the high-grained broncho to drink several times in the crossing, as he certainly would not have done had he been riding far that night. By this time the animal would have been frightened into a fit by such treatment, had it known the Apache as the Apache knew the horse.

Don-Ha rode toward Placid's teepee. From a distance he heard the oxhide drum; also as he approached, several ponies nickered excitedly, his own lifting its head to answer, but Don-Ha stopped the racket by closing his fingers over the beast's windpipe. Ahead, the tethered ponies threshed about at his coming—four of them near the door of Placid's teepee, one or two crazy with thirst and hunger. They had been tethered long already. Don-Ha dismounted, fastened his own mount securely with the others and left it there, going back to his own place on foot.

The next day he went about his affairs as usual, but that night after long sitting by the fire, instead of spreading his pallet, he arose and made his way back toward Placid's lodge. Within three hundred yards, he stalked it as if reconnoitering an enemy's camp. He listened to the drum-beats and fixed his eyes at length on the firelight and watched long. A white man could have seen at most only an occasional stir of shadows in the distance, but Don-Ha saw all that he was looking for. There were now but three ponies in front of Placid's lodge. One of these was his own—having by this time been tethered there nearly thirty hours.

He continued silently to watch. At last a human figure came out from the teepee and moved among the ponies, stopped in front of his, loosened and led it away to water. Two other figures came and removed the two other ponies. They were seen no more, but his was brought back and fed; this by no other than the narrow cool hands of Placid herself.

After a half-hour, she tied up a great bundle of grama grass, gave it to a younger brother to carry, and started in Don-Ha's direction, leading the pony. Silently he arose and drew back before her, making no sound of stone or twig as he retreated. He was back in his teepee with the tongue drawn, and lying in the trampled grass inside, one eye pressing out under the folds, when Placid appeared.

She halted, looked about, presently fastened the pony near his door, opened the pile of dried grass at the tether-post and departed.

This was the acceptance of Don-Ha by the sister of Lost Pony. The other suitors had their answer by being forced to come and take back their own ponies. Had Placid watered and fed and led back Don-Ha's pony sooner, she would have shown an unwonted eagerness to be married; had she tarried beyond the second night she would have appeared too proud.

The marriage ceremony began at once. Old warriors foregathered at the teepee of Placid's parents and began recounting adventures and exploits, each man telling his own, for he knew that best, drinking tizwin and such fierier ministrations as were afforded. Meanwhile Don-Ha conferred with the girl's father, a bargaining arrangement, but neatly and not greedily conducted. Horses were money and Placid was no one-horse affair. She came high—a string of five, in fact, but Old Man Parent knew that the more he demanded, the more his daughter would be appreciated.

Placid at this time was in the hands of the old wives, being instructed in the ways and duties of married women—wisdom won from much sorrow, canniness wrung from parturition; experiences, knowledges to a nicety, in the precarious secrets of manhandling as a life work. Placid listened and listened, the hair of her eyebrows having been plucked out meanwhile, and seven thin red lines painted from her lower lip down to the base of her chin.

The climax of all knowledge imparted to Placid was the story of the great sex schism told by Calico Turkey herself, the story of that day when squaws, without a single one holding back, left the teepees of the males and crossed the Big River. Only squaws were permitted to listen to this cherished revelation as Wano-boono told it. In fact, through the entire festival Don-Ha was not permitted within reach of Placid's hand. The first day of the marriage feast passed; another night and day, still another night—Don-Ha and Placid still held apart from each other. It was a matter of waiting between old and young. There could be but one end to such a battle, for the young waited for a prize and the old had nothing to wait for but sleep. For three full days the endurance match lasted, until the last drunken and exhausted squaw dozed deeper and deeper. Then the lovers moved swiftly out of the sated festival.

IX

D ON-HA perceived that to take the easier way to put a
thing out of mind is to bind it to you; that one drags it
after him thereafter. Again he sat alone by the fire in
the evening, and called for his pallet outside, instead of
entering the teepee when his solitary ruminations were
over.

This was aspersion on Placid, but she was cool in the
head as well as in person. She was treated well; she had
heard too much from the squaws not to know that in
most ways she was well off. Moreover, she knew something of the quiet force as well as the obvious strength
of her lord. This entitled him to eccentricity; so long as
he did not break the bond, she would not. She knew he
was dissatisfied with her, but also that no woman in the
village could have held his thoughts for long from himself. She was by no means dead in the head as she carried
her first baby, and a way formed to make him see her
values.

Don-Ha's thoughts were not clear and manageable as
before; new forces aroused in him that distracted his
thoughts like distant war-drums. He was nettled with
complication and blamed Placid for not being enough, so
that he could easily fall back into his old self again. He
wanted to brood in the old undistracted way on the doing
of great future deeds among men; to practice make-believe
thoughts of being one who already undisputed chieftain,
but the institution of householding and husbandry was
now alive in his life. He heard the hubbub of squaws

and ninyas in the evening as he had not heard such sounds before.

There was one of the family of Soldado Fiero, a small dark tongue of flame. As a slip of a girl she had been humorously called Ish-kay-nay. This means "boy" and she was nicknamed so because she could do most of the things boys do. Among the females, she was the fastest runner in the tribe; few bucks could pass her for a short distance. Her name now was Ko-do, the Firefly, and for reasons which the squaws knew, there was a whisper afloat concerning her, having to do with the nature of the glowworm. Placid permitted Don-Ha to hear squaw talk to the effect that Firefly was one set apart; that not one man in a thousand could know the secret of her.

Don-Ha considered this deeply. It had perhaps something to do with the girl's father, Soldado Fiero, a small dark man past forty, always an adviser for raids and wars, a great rider and killer, a devilish Apache, well thought of. A man's blood was everything in the nature of offspring. Don-Ha considered Soldado's sons—Pindah, the eldest, much cherished for speed, malice, and still more for cunning; his friend, Black Knife and also others, far-riding scourges, never particularly friendly to himself, nor he with them. Yet he would have picked them for dangerous adventure.

Firefly was a friend of Placid. She often came over from the inner camp. She passed close to his solitary fire like as not in the evening. Once she shied like a filly when he skited a handful of gravel at her feet. She had seemed to rise from the earth in the dusk, and the sound she made in her throat kept repeating in his brain that night—a wild·breathless "ca-a-h-h."

Another dusk as he sat outside, Firefly came and vanished into the teepee where Placid was. He heard the two laughing. He felt them laughing at him. This was not good. It filled him with thick red vapors, as if he were swimming to the eyes. Then Placid went out for water or wood and Firefly was there alone. Don-Ha considered, but was in no mood for clear thinking, no solid ground for his thoughts to stand upon. Firefly was in there alone, where the scent of dried grass blent with the garments and affairs of women. She was in there in the stifling dark. She was cupped, captured like a mouse in a gourd.

He moved toward the single opening. He felt like a wall of black cloud with a fork of lightning in the center. He could see her in the dark.

It was like the last nine miles to water—those three, five steps—until his hands closed upon her. Not a sound, as his hands crushed upon the blades of her shoulders. She went still as a bird in a serpent spell—until his strength brought the throaty "ca-a-h-h," this time breathed upon his own lips, and he backed out with an image of Firefly in his heart, sitting there, a lasting mischief, and the fiery taste of her in his mouth.

Surely the mother of Firefly had been struck by lightning in her bearing-time.

The whole thing was gone through again within two years of his first marriage feast. Shortly thereafter he came to know that a man who would give his undivided attention to his own future, as the master of tribal affairs, must guard himself well from the clutches of women; that to be chief of a household is one thing and chief of a tribe quite another. Much thinking about the institution of husbandry in this period netted certain small facts;

He had not chosen Placid in the first place, but had opened to her in listening to her brother. He had not really chosen Firefly; the whole thing having been arranged between her and Placid, and he had walked into their net thinking he was a great man.

Placid had chosen Firefly for her second as a foil for herself—the one among all Mimbreno women who would make what she was more desirable—like cool milk after fiery peppers. He knew now what the squaws had meant and that they were laughing at him for having taken a slakeless fever for a woman—glowworm.

There were the seeds for further deeper ponderings:

That where man's cunning ends woman's cunning merely begins, that woman is the real enemy to man; that a man who can master woman must first master himself, which is not fully required in the mastering of men; that one who gives his thought to the mastering of women will find the problems of men very simple in contrast.

He now had a house with two sides. This was not good. He used it only for days of storm or rain. The steam of cooking is well enough, or the steam of caves when one is sick, but a house that hisses with steam from two women who are fire and water to each other—was no place for a man to be.

And again Don-Ha was seen to sit by his own fire, and to gather his robes about him for sleep where he sat. And already he was considering a way to stop the laughter of the two in his teepee and the laughter of other squaws when he came near.

X

THESE things gradually died out in importance and Don-Ha was himself again more than ever, still putting two and two together in his thoughts. Except that he had seen Aña, a Mexican girl, in a house neighboring to the Padre's mission in Santa Rita—frightened fascinated eyes occasionally lifted his way from her washing—he was more than ever lost in the affairs of men. Two of Placid's children were now underfoot, but Ko-do, the Firefly, gave no signs of being other than herself.

It was now a critical time of his life in the tribe; he was due to take a step forward in the minds of men, to fix his place as warrior with an act that would be remembered. He had to think of making his name. The Mimbrenos were not at war, so the thing that he chose pertained to the arts of peace.

Soccoro—maize.

The Medicine Padre was responsible for this. It was a thing the Padre had suggested repeatedly. Because of many words from the Padre; because he knew how, from working occasionally in the Padre's garden, Don-Ha was actually brought to scratching the ground for himself. The squaws could not do it, not even bring water until he showed them how. It is true that he heard laughter behind him as he worked, and fancied the whispered word "Pima" or "Opata" (spoken with a slap on the haunch). None dared to speak to him directly. He had only to straighten up and they leaped back like startled colts. He was keenly respected in his own set, and judgment upon the thing he was doing was mainly reserved. This is the Apache way. If one thinks out a thing, the thought is not judged, but the action that comes of it. If that fails, caste is lost.

Don-Ha could bide his time and say nothing because he foresaw bags of corn in his teepee as in the stone granaries of the Nakai-yes for the winter, and browned hoe-cakes out of the ash for his own breakfast frosty mornings when other braves chewed mesquite beans.

The planting of corn held him, even against his pride. He did not care to let others see how interested he was, for the thing had witchcraft about it—seedlings coming up in his own patch. He would have bent over them a lot more than he did, but for others watching. Never was there anything like those little spears coming up to order in the place he had set.

He felt himself going out to them—like a loss of virtue. His thoughts were pulled to the corn patch when he was not there. If anyone touched that, they touched him. This was not good. A man was not rightly himself, spread out over a corn patch like this. Of course, he did little or none of the work after the planting. His squaws did that, but still his thoughts were pinned to the corn patch—like a deerskin to a tree. He was not himself.

That was a long summer. None other was like it. Planting and seedlings were one thing, but long weeks another. Father Font came to see the patch, and watched it like a new church being built. It was a church—built by many, many words. It was also part of the Bridge— corn, the man-taming, blood-bought corn.

First the gophers came, and ate up through the ground to the very root-crowns, leaving a lopped stalk; then the rabbits came in from the desert and could not believe their eyes. This was fit to die for. Finally the birds came. Don-Ha and his two squaws were pelted with laughter.

Because his thought had not matured into healthy result—not even one bag of corn for the winter—Don-Ha lost face with his people. The act which he had chosen made him lose caste instead of gaining it. To fail in what one undertakes is a black mark with the tribe. It does not matter that one learns from the error. The mistake alone counts. One has not turned it over again and again in the mind sufficiently.

To waste one's self in work is another black mark. So much for the Padre's soccoro idea. So much for that plank of the Bridge. And Don-Ha was speckled hot all over his body where his pride broke out in explosive rash.

And this was what all his listening and thinking had done for him—to make him less than others instead of more. Very narrowly he escaped getting his tribal name just there. It was because there were several names being considered—Rabbit Fighter—Corn Watcher—Water Carrier—that one of them did not settle for good. If any name as sweepingly descriptive as Scare Crow had occurred, it would doubtless have settled and stuck, but that had never been heard of.

It was more than ever a critical time for Don-Ha. Some great thing must now be done. He had two steps to make, where one would have sufficed before. One step to regain lost ground; that is, to make the corn patch as if it were not in the mind of a people whose memory is its long suite; another step up into the graces of a people reluctant to grant any particular significance to its youth.

One morning of early spring before dawn, he emerged

from his teepee, and walked out among the tethered ponies. He placed one hand on the withers, another on the rump of a paint-horse, as if he were feeling its workmanship. Then he slithered up and guided the beast out of camp with his knees.

He was gone many days—one whole moon and well into the bulge of another. He was following a thought that resulted from words overheard in Santa Rita del Cobre; one of the first practical results of his trained ear for Spanish. In the matter of soccoro, he had used private knowledge also, but this must be managed better than that. He came back to the Copper Mines empty-handed, without even the horse he took away, but that was merely accentuation of the fact that he was very rich, indeed.

XI

THE overheard word was to the effect that a party of white trappers, not Spaniards, but of a fabled race far to the Northwest, had been operating all winter in the high creeks beyond the Big River in the upper ranges of the Mescalero country. Moreover, this word proved true. Don-Ha located the party* after five suns and disposed of his horse as he came near. From a glittering pinnacle he made out four lanky, bearded strangers and one boy. His movements thereafter were conducted with consummate caution. The Mexicans had spoken of these whites with a manner of respect which must mean they knew what they were doing at all times. In fact, Don-Ha operated as he would if a band of his own people had been under surveillance. This was compliment indeed to the strangers. Besides, he had no wish to encounter a bright Mescalero eye.

The trappers had two mules which he gave a wide berth. A mule not inured to Indian camps is dangerous to an Apache, smelling the Indian even farther than strange dogs.

Don-Ha hovered for days above the camps of the strangers, often following them one by one along the creeks. They had their winter furs cached variously and had done well. They took the small animals with great skill, and sat and smoked about their fire in the evening, making flour pancakes that smelled differently from the tortillas of the Mexicans. Four white men and a boy.

---

*The Pattie party, 1824.

One of the men was pale and old, his chin whiskers the color of white iron. He was the father of the boy and leader of the group. Don-Ha called him Chawn-clizzay, meaning the goat, on account of his face-hair.

What the secretive observer approved most in his unrelenting studies was the marksmanship of the trappers. At the full distance of two arrows they brought down deer or wild pig. He saw one of the trappers drop a drinking deer to its knees far down a ravine, a distance of several minutes' running, and this shot lived in his mind all his years. They shot bears as readily as anything else; this being against the Apache morale. Also they ate fish, the smell of their evening camp on these occasions, sending the watcher farther off in disgust. They often played with little cards in the firelight. One by one they would lay out an equal number to each with great ceremony; then pick them up together and look long. After consideration, they would lay them down one by one each in his turn, until the crack began in the game; then one of the men would choose one card remaining and thrash it down on the blanket as if to break it, with hawhaws and a spoken phrase now becoming familiar to the listener, though it was not Spanish. Then they would begin quietly again, no thought of being watched, whatever.

No Spaniards ever shot as they did. With a gun like that and the power to shoot like that, Don-Ha perceived he could have brought the trappers down one by one and never once been seen. He could have destroyed them one by one with arrows, but he had not come for that. No one of his own people had ever watched like this, nor learned the ways of strangers, nor listened to their voices. Days passed very quickly. He covered all his own signs and kept one eye over his shoulder for Mescaleros. When he craved roasted flesh, he retired to a distant canyon where his fire could not be seen. There was some of his horse still left in dried strips when he did not risk a fire.

One day the party gathered up all the traps and forded the Big River, moving west toward the Copper Mines. Now Don-Ha began to be troubled that he had waited too long. He had not counted on them ceasing all work in the creeks so abruptly. They had left nothing behind and were not separated through the days as aforetime. The mules were heavily laden, the days becoming very warm. The watcher had learned much, but that was not all he had come for. In the absorption of his studies he had not forgotten the thing he was required to do to obliterate the soccoro folly. Rather he had renewed in his ponderings night and morning the primary purpose of his setting out.

It looked bad now. The trappers were making a passage. They appeared to be heading for the Copper Mines, although there was no trading post there to dispose of such a quantity of furs. Each morning they set out early and traveled the full day. Within two suns from Santa Rita they tethered their mules and brought forage instead of turning the animals loose as usual for the night. That meant an extra early start and possibly a longer jornada tomorrow, which would bring them to camp well in the Apache stronghold tomorrow night. Don-Ha surveyed with self-displeasure the many chances he had missed in days past.

The next day they traveled rapidly until mid-afternoon and came to halt in a dim and rocky canyon he knew very well indeed. All this district was deeply cut with ravines, and the Mimbrenos spoke of it as the Dark Canyons. He was in doubt for a time why they had stopped so early. It was not for food. Chawn-clizzay took a position in the rim of the canyon; the other three and the boy set about unpacking and clearing away rock and earth for a deep hole. If they were really making a cache, this was more than he could ask. They worked into the dark and Don-Ha was so intensely occupied with watching that he forgot his own hunger and lay close until their fire was black.

Next morning they were very silent about finishing their work. When it was done they started off, leaving no guard, their voices louder, freer. They took but a few furs and showed well pleased at the thought of a day's rest with the miners of Santa Rita. Chawn-clizzay sat one of the mules. The other carried the small bale of furs. These were for exchange, doubtless for fresh supplies. Now it was evident that they meant to take their winter's work to Janos or Tubac, and did not want the Mimbrenos to know how rich they were.

That was a very busy day for Don-Ha. He did the work of two mules, also the work of the four men and a boy, in digging and carrying. It was squaws' work, too, much of it; but there would be ample time to make up for that. The trappers had cached well, but Don-Ha knew a far better cache, one of his own private banks of boyhood days. It was not far, but he reached it circuitously, familiarizing himself with details of the treasure in the numerous loads. At nightfall, there was upon him the smell of all the fur-bearing animals of the Apache habitat—to be washed and smoked from his body and garments, before he cared to darken the triangle of his own teepee.

XII

For a moment at his own doorway he stood bowed, castdown in the dawn. Placid came out, sleep still fleeing from her eyes and looked at his empty hands and tattered moccasins. Her eye filled with the fact that he had brought no horses, not even one for the one taken away. Meanwhile, she was broad awake and stirring about as if he had come in rich from solitary warpath. The papooses squawked and the beady eyes of Firefly showed at the curtain. Silently he ate, and kept on eating and drinking until the sun was high.

The camp showed no surprise at his return. More miners had come to Santa Rita del Cobre; more dust and racket from their tunneling. Soldado Fiero had headed south in a raid; Juan Jose was drunk in Santa Rita. Don-Ha was informed that a party of white eyes called "Meh-hi-kanos" had come in yesterday with two tall mules and a bundle of fox and beaver pelts of the size one squaw could carry. They were feasting and drinking in Santa Rita as if they had skinned the territory. Also it was in a way no Spaniards ever drank and feasted. Four white men with bushy faces and one boy with hair under his hat only.

Don-Ha went to the village to see. It was quite true. The "Meh-hi-kanos" were drinking fast and eating one meal on top of another. Old Chawn-clizzay did not drink, but sat apart and smiled. Mexicans called him, "Senor Pat-tee." He seemed very tired and weak. The boy did not drink. Senoritas played with the three trappers. Don-Ha heard the senoritas speak of them as "Los Go-dammies." This was from the words they spoke so frequently—the same which Don-Ha had often heard in the upper camps over the card-play, or when shots killed or did not kill. Also when traps were well filled or not filled.

Don-Ha watched them closely, appearing to doze. He had not seen them closely like this. He closely examined their shirts, faces, breeches, boots, belts, knives; especially he examined their undershirts and the rifles they had brought with them. They were greatly to be respected for their use of pesh-e-gar. No Spaniard was to be respected to the same degree. The strangers, in fact, stirred him vaguely but constantly; he knew much of them, more of them than any of his people, but something he did not know ached and stirred within him. In fact, Don-Ha thought very well of the white trappers, except for their foolishness in caching their treasures in a land created for a people that uses its eyes.

All Santa Rita forgot its customary ways to entertain and study the bearded strangers. The senoritas came out to the little plaza before noon and swung their hips past the shop doors where they sat drinking, quite as if the sun were going down. Their dresses were freshly washed —legs covered to the stiff sabatos they walked in so noisily. Whenever the strangers laughed, the senoritas were affected, even at a distance, and clung to one another excitedly. There was one senorita, however, who did not come to the plaza in daylight.

Don-Ha arose at length and went to the Mission, but the Medicine Padre was away in Janos or elsewhere. No vino or cafe to be gotten there, no food with peppers.

But that one senorita was washing her clothes in the side
of the house near the Mission. For some time he watched
her from the little patio of the Medicine Padre, until she
felt his eyes and vanished. He considered that the Nakai-
yes were very dirty to require so much washing. He
studied the prints of her bare feet in the dust before the
tubs, and fitted her feet to them in his thoughts, and
regarded the white flowers at her doorstep in passing.

No food or drink to be gotten in the shops of Santa Rita
either, unless one paid the price for it, which was confusing. On the contrary there was tuh-le-pah in his home
camp. Besides, back among his people again, it was good
to sleep.

The next morning he was told that the white trappers
had returned the way they came, to which he nodded
merely, as to squaw talk of little importance. Nor did
he betray interest late in afternoon when the trappers
were seen coming back down the mountain very wrathful
and dangerous. Dogs were barking over all the presidio;
dogs in the Indian camp had taken it up. The Mimbrenos murmured as at the coming of the strangers on
the war-path.

"Tuh-le-pah!" grunted Don-Ha, and Placid brought a
brimming gourdful, spilling some of it in her concern not
to miss what was happening. This she ran away to do.
Don-Ha drowsed. One had to drink much tuh-le-pah to
make up for little mescal, but plenty tuh-le-pah made for
fine entertainment among one's thoughts, while plenty
mescal made one feel like burning up the village. Placid
returned, having ascertained that the trappers had found
their cache rifled; that they had brought but a small por-

tion of their furs the first time, that the rest had been stolen to the last hair, and many things besides.

"Tuh-le-pah!" grunted Don-Ha and saw the beady eyes of Firefly fixed upon him from the tongue of the teepee. He fell to thinking of her and her people—Soldado Fiero away on a hunting raid which the Mexicans of Santa Rita would hear about presently—Black Knife with him. It was a great problem that one always had to be missed from camp when things like this occurred. One could not be seen in camp as usual while great things were going on at a distance. Soldado would likely bring back many horses.

"I myself brought back no horses," thought Don-Ha.

Horses were good.

But it would be known that Soldado Fiero was away from his camp when these things happened in the lower villages. Still it was better to be the life of Soldado than to be the life of Juan Jose. It was Juan Jose's weakness in the beginning that permitted the miners to return to the Copper Mines. This was freely granted. Still, there would have been no Santa Rita del Cobre otherwise. Much had happened for good and ill because of that. The Mimbrenos were not the same; there were two bands instead of one. The squaws were wanting many things like the Mexican women; papooses were picking up Spanish words. Life was not the same. There was much drinking among the Apaches of Juan Jose's band. Drink was very easy.

Still tuh-le-pah was good, plenty tuh-le-pah.

There was another side, however. With no Santa Rita, there would have been no Spanish to talk and listen to; no senoritas to examine closely and at a distance; there would have been no Medicine Padre to go to, no senorita in the doorway near by the Padre's patio. There would have been no corn folly, either. That was true. There would have been no words overheard about the white trappers hunting in the high creeks at the edge of the neighboring Mescaleros. Life would have been one thing with Juan Jose a strong man; as it was, life was quite another.

He saw the beady eyes of Firefly in the teepee flap again. She was a coiling viper, a striking viper. At least none other had her, however.

"Tuh-le-pah," he called, and she did not hurry to bring it. The time would come when he would press a fire-thorn into the quick of her heel, so she would jump when spoken to.

Placid returned with the words that Santa Rita mescal shops were bolting their doors against the trappers and all the senoritas running to the mission.

XIII

O NE DAY Don-Ha went to the bank. He had not hurried to do this. The noise of the trappers had long died down; the dust of their trail to Tubac long since settled. He went to the bank but not directly; first to the camp of Soldado Fiero where he sat a full day, listening to Apache deeds among the big mountains to the south. His eyes filled with the new horses one by one. They were good. Black Knife had much to tell. Don-Ha had sadly missed by not going along. There was much disagreement in the camp of Soldado Fiero with the ways of Juan Jose, and with the life of the "village" Mimbrenos. Juan Jose was not given to great ranging jornados as aforetime, his people would soon be living in clay houses like the Mexicans.

Then Don-Ha moved on as if toward the Big River. Presently he turned north around the Springs, and in the night reached his bank—where he sat on the rim of the canyon until day broke, until the shadows were driven away in all directions, and he was alone, no doubt whatsoever. Then he concerned himself with matters of principal and interest for many hours, broken only by intervals of watching. At nightfall he moved back the way he had come, to the Warm Springs and the camp of Soldado Fiero. Woven in the crook of his elbow as the trappers carried the same, was a long gleaming flintlock— pesh-e-gar, the rifle — the first that had ever been brought into the camp of Soldado for smell-and-touch examination.

Now Don-Ha stood unconcerned while Mimbreno eyes concentrated upon this bright engine fashioned by the very gods of covetousness. Yes, it would shoot. Don-Ha showed them. Not very small or far the target, but he showed them, knowing a peculiar sickness of having less powder and ball after each shot, with no way of making more, as with arrows.

Then Don-Ha sat down to meat, with the remark that he was running low on horses; in fact, that he was pretty near out of horses. Black Knife brought his father, Soldado himself. Would Don-Ha care to trade pesh-e-gar for horses, several horses, many horses?

No, Don-Ha would not, but while recently abroad, at the same time Soldado Fiero was abroad on rich raiding, he had gathered together a bundle of furs, as much as a squaw could carry. These he would exchange for suitable horses—some fox and beaver and cougar pelts, but not many.

At this time Black Knife and his father and other warriors were looking upon Don-Ha as a man suddenly grown. The manner of his carrying the flintlock was that of a great man, and the strange garment protruding from the sleeves of his hunting shirt was much to be prized. Moreover, when a bundle of rare furs of highest quality was brought, it became clear that many common furs must be held back; all of which connected the mind with the story of the trappers' cache, a subject of fruitless pondering these many days. Soldado Fiero and his sons and warriors considered that Don-Ha doubtless had several rifles in hiding, and that it would be well to negotiate ungreedily with one who single-handed had wrought so great a thing. This in the light of further transactions.

Moreover, was not this vastly-proportioned young warrior the son of Soldado Fiero himself by marriage to Firefly? And the brother of Pindah, Black Knife and the others? Should such an one be of low degree in the matter of horses?

So it was that with tidings going before him, Don-Ha rode back to his own teepees with four ponies trailing the one he had saddled, and the gleaming rifle across his arm as the trappers carried the same when mule-sitting.

Nor was that all. The beady eyes of Firefly were first to fix upon the utterly handsome forearms of her lord— sleeves of a shirt of bright red wool, protruding from under his hunting shirt—flaming wool of the incredible fascination of turkey red—protruding sleeves, very hot, indeed. They bulged the eyeball to fullness and the point of pain, second only to pesh-e-gar passing from hand to hand among the braves.

Now Don-Ha was connected with the plight of the trappers in exceeding great honor, the more especially in the camp of Juan Jose's Mimbrenos since he alone, one man, had accomplished as much, more perhaps, than the entire raiding party of Soldado Fiero. But none of these things were spoken in Don-Ha's presence. It was not the custom.

And Don-Ha himself was not through. His thought was only partly carried out.

In fact, the main idea, conceived in the low-down time following the corn patch, was still up his sleeve. Moreover, the bulk of his treasure, hardly touched yet, was still in the bank, where it could not remain too long with heat of high summer creeping into the ground.

XIV

D on-Ha moved his squaws up toward the bank, but not too near, and set them to work salvaging and tanning through the summer. Even they saw only what he showed them of his treasure, and knew only what he told them, which was less. The further steps of the affair he had in mind had to wait for the Medicine Padre, who did not come to Santa Rita for the present, being unable to travel in the great heat. Still Don-Ha watched another in Santa Rita who had part in his plan, and nourished the whole with daily thinking.

Meanwhile his position in both Apache camps was nicely enhanced. The more warriors thought of it, step by step, the more commendation grew. The steps of his action were dear to all Mimbrenos, because of the matured success of each thought. Especially was Don-Ha approved for his coming empty-handed to his squaws, and for his unobtrusive study of the trappers at close range as they drank in Santa Rita before discovering their loss.

They approved of his continence in speech. Of his power to contain himself, evidence was further given by Don-Ha that summer. He had brought a few tanned pelts into Santa Rita to be exchanged for coined money; not "cobre" such as was sent down into Mexico in the crude from these very mines, but white iron—very difficult to possess. Though Don-Ha bargained carefully that day, he was not given what he expected for the pelts. White iron was never given so. No matter what one considered one's property to be worth as one brought it to

Santa Rita, it was always worth less. On the other hand, the trading power of a little silver was exceeding great. Much thinking did not altogether simplify these things.

Don-Ha had received his silver for the pelts; all too little, but it was good. Then he was asked to drink, which was price in addition and not to be taken lightly. There was the trader himself and another Mexican.

He was asked to drink again—mescal poured large and freely. The Mexican spoke of more pelts. Don-Ha said he would go north to the snows this coming winter. If the winter were cold perhaps the creatures would put on heavy furs. The two Mexicans laughed loudly at this and poured more mescal. Don-Ha felt the heat in his veins and the powers of ready speech on his lips, yet speech that came freely often lacked the wisdom of thoughts that one had gone over again and again. Don-Ha cared not for such speech, save to listen to it from others.

Then one of the Mexicans asked how many white men Don-Ha would have working for him among his traps this coming winter, and did not wait for his answer loudly to laugh. Don-Ha watched them in silence, appearing not to comprehend. At heart he was undisturbed. It is one thing to be thought a man of great prowess, and another to confess it. The most foolish of all Mimbrenos would not have dared to speak to him directly of his engagement with the white trappers, and these Mexicans were not entitled to straight words from Apache lips.

So Don-Ha more carefully contained his liquor, wondering why so much mescal was spent after he had already been paid for his pelts. Nor did he touch his own silver in that shop; little enough had been received in the first place. All this talk and laughter did no harm, with firewater in abundance as never before. Finally one of the Mexicans looked out the doorway saying that night was falling and that the door should be shut. The other agreed to this and Don-Ha drank with them in candle-light, the two Mexicans laughing and talking like great men.

The fire in his brain burned low. It was always so with much drink, but the fire in his belly burned high, filling him full of powers that cried to be used. He wanted to rise and talk; he wanted to wrestle with them and show them his strength, but all the more he stayed still. Then, as well as if they had spoken it in his own tongue, he saw now what they meant to do—to take his money when he fell asleep. He would wake up and pat his breech-cloth for his money and it would be gone.

Still he did not move. He was holding to the thoughts in his head, against all the burning incentives of his flesh. And this he did until the Mexicans went limp before him, so that there was no danger. Don-Ha sat drinking alone after they slid to the floor; then he arose and hunched his shoulders and felt the floor under his feet and walked out softly—walking far out in the mesquite, because he had to be sick, a thing to be done alone.

Later he fell asleep in the cover of the mesquite with the moon splintering through. He awoke and it was not the moon but the sun through the branches. He changed this position and slept again, until the sickness was gone from him and he was hungry and athirst. His hand reached to his breech-cloth, and there was the deerskin wallet untouched, exactly the price of the furs remaining with him. He returned to the village and went to the

Mission, inquiring for the return of the Medicine Padre. Today he was told that Father Font would soon be on the way from Janos. In a nearby doorway he saw a face seen many times before at the washtub—frightened, fascinated eyes. He made no sign. In the market place, he bought provisions and mescal and took these to his own teepee where he feasted alone, the squaws being still absent.

XV

Soon afterward, the squaws returned and the Medicine Padre had come again to Santa Rita. Don-Ha straightened himself under the dimming stars of early morning. From his little pouch of hoddentin, he took forth a pinch of the powder, and blew it toward the dark east; another pinch he blew toward Santa Rita del Cobre. This was for additional good fortune to attend his thoughts which were to become action this day. Then he straightened his sleeves, caught a pony and rode into the village, smelling the houses with dislike. They always made him feel less than himself, like a prison closing around him, so that it was with effort that he kept the rod of his purpose upstanding. All, however, had been fully thought out. He smelled the mescal in the closed shops; he smelled the meats and vegetables, boots and lamp oil, a seething mass of smells with the town-smell over all.

The dogs barked at him, but that was always so. Indian dogs barked at the Mexicans when they approached the Apache camps. Nearing the mission, he passed the pickets of a certain 'dobe house, with low masses of white flowers at the doorstep. His pony was now pulled to a slow dragging walk—soundless in the dust.

He was ready, but no one else was ready. He stopped near the low mission building, left his pony at the rail and moved softly in back where the Padre lived. The old man was still asleep. His snoring could be heard through the blinds. Snoring was not good. One who

snored on the warpath could never go far with other
braves, nor a man who sneezed unexpectedly. Such men
were in the class of horses that stumbled. Don-Ha
squatted down on the stones near a gutter under the
eaves. The earth was cold to the flesh, but his bones
were warm; the sun came up and warmed his flesh. A
fire burned steadily in his brain. Nothing disturbed it.
The Padre's servant came out and found him there.
"Madre de Deo!"—she bolted in and began laying the
fire. He smelled coffee soon and licked his thin wide
lips.

"Cafe—buen."

A cup was brought to him. He waited a little for it
to cool and emptied it in one pouring. Another was
brought. Coffee was good.

The saintly Padre was making morning sounds in his
little cell of a room, cleaning his pipes as do those who
sleep indoors. He opened the lattice. "Buenas Dias,
Don-Ha!" he called and moved on into the church to say
his morning mass before breaking his fast.

The Mimbreno had only once entered the church. It
made him feel like that cave where one could not walk
without hearing steps behind him. He never entered
the Medicine Padre's quarters. He did not like the smell
of dusty books and saturated drains. He did not like the
smell of the Padre himself—the smell of white sweat,
he called it.

The sun was coming up when the Padre returned.
"Have some coffee, Don-Ha," he said.

"Cafe—buen," said Don-Ha.

"Make more coffee, Euphemia," said the priest.

"Drink your own. I am making more," she answered,

and added in rapid lingo, all of which the guest could not catch, "This Indian bull never stops—"

"Do as I ask you," said the Padre.

The servant brought the Padre's chair outside. They sat down against the west wall facing the sun. As the wall warmed, the Padre leaned back, but Don-Ha sat straight and still. His back straight, immense, with legs partly covered, gave him the look of a prodigious cripple. His right sleeve showed, the vivid red of new wool. More coffee was brought. Don-Ha smoked in silence until words slowly warmed within him. The Padre knew this time he should keep his own words back. Finally Don-Ha began:

"Long time sit here. Much time pass. Medicine Padre speak many words. Indian listen—no speak. Now Indian speak to good friend."

"That is well, Don-Ha."

"Friends speak what is in the heart—no fear."

"No fear between friends, Don-Ha."

The Padre eyed the red sleeve as he waited. The new wool tightly fitted the mighty right arm to the very wrist.

"Today Indian take Mexican girl to Indian teepee."

"What girl, Don-Ha?"

The Apache pointed over his shoulder to the neighbor's house. He had heard the name "Aña" many times, but for some reason did not try to say it. It was not the name he thought of her with.

"Surely you would not take Aña from her parents!"

"Long time wait. She is ready now."

"She has told you she is ready to go with you, Don-Ha?"

"No speak. Make her like—when she come."

"You have never once spoken to her?"

"No speak. See her long time. Go way—make ready. Today I myself come."

"When did you think of this first?"

"Long time ago—little girl."

"It will make trouble for many people, Don-Ha."

"Indian strong like many people pull together. Indian come first to tell friend."

The Padre was silent. He was plenty warm now. There was moisture upon his brow. His face was pale, his eyes sad, but different from ever before. The Padre felt traces of anger, the first time in many years, but old training held. Under the surge of anger he had learned long ago not to speak. There was no steady light where gusts of anger were possible. Yet the trouble mounted blacker and blacker as he thought.

Years of patient labor had only amounted to this—the making of a prince of trouble-makers in this village of his parish. Knowledges and countless hours of talk and food-passing had amounted to this: the bringing about of the very triumph of trouble-making that no other Apache could think of.

He knew what happened to Mexican girls with Apaches; that their condition was a slavery worse than death. He knew the power of the squaws, that they would permit no equality; that their vanity was stimulated by the presence of a foreigner; that they, the servants and burden-bearers of their own camp, became the cruelest masters imaginable to one lower than they. He knew that no foreign influence is permitted to come between two Apache warriors; that the law of the tribe worked in every way possible to prevent internecine strife. He had seen a horse, claimed by two warriors, deliberately shot by a head man to settle the dispute, and a girl slave given to a third or become public property, because two braves claimed her.

He had known Aña always. Better death than this. The anger surged through him again, darker and hotter than before. He covered his face. All the years had not eradicated the enemy from his own blood. It was true with him what aspirants of old had found—that the snake of the self had merely gone pale from long fasting and still lived within him. He who prayed for others now prayed silently for himself—that he might be able to do now what he had told others so often and so long to do.

His eyes opened. He saw the great-bodied buck— Apache, the word that means Enemy—Apache, by name and nature. All the years of bending to this one in cultivation, years of watering, of forcing—had brought upon him this devilish thing.

Then he began to know a strange thought. He began to know in part what it had meant to Don-Ha to bring word of his intention before action. It was un-Apache. It was unprecedented. The Padre saw that he knew nothing of Apache nature after all; that all his years he had used a white man's psychology upon a red man and that it did not fit any more than the pelt of a bear would fit the body of an ox. One might as well try to teach a bear or an ox in terms of man's understanding . . . yet this Apache had come to him first. He did not come to ask, to advise. He had come to tell his decision. Don-Ha would do as he said; no mortal power could dissuade him. Even so the Padre's heart began to soften. Don-Ha had come to him first. This was Apache fealty—

"I wish you would not do this thing, Don-Ha—"

The other answered in his own language because he knew no Spanish equivalent for the meaning in his mind: "It is as good as done," or as one would say, "It is already wrapped up and delivered."

"Aña's parents will fight and kill your people. They will send for the soldiers at Janos."

Don-Ha paused. Then he spoke a sentence in his own language. "Dih asd-za hig-e balgon-ya-hi dont-e shilg-nli dah," because he could not put it in Spanish. Literally he conveyed, "This I have done and what has resulted therefrom is all the same to me." He added in Spanish:

"Mimbreno Indian not afraid Mexican soldier. Indian don't care for Mexican miner in his country. Mexican here no good for Apache-man; no good for Apache squaw; no good for Apache papoose."

"Does Juan Jose know of this thing?" the Padre asked finally.

"No. Indian come to tell his friend first."

"The village will be open to you no more."

"Men who are brothers are not broken in friendship by the things of women—"

"I am Aña's friend, too. I am the friend of her father and her mother. They are of my people."

"This Indian is your friend. He does not come to steal. He comes to tell before he takes. He comes to his friend first."

"That is true, Don-Ha. You make it very hard. Can you not wait until I think—see clearly—prepare the way?"

"I am ready. She is ready. I come for her soon."

"It will make bad blood. It will bring death!"

"Indian strong like many people."

"Your own people will not like it!"

"Indian make his people like it!"

"Your own women, Don-Ha—what will they say?"

"Indian brave does not listen to women."

"But they will make a slave of Aña!"

"I do not bring senorita to my teepee for a slave."

"But when you are away they will flog and torture her. It has been done."

"They will be flogged and tortured. It is not for slave that senorita comes to Indian teepee. I myself rule my own house. She will have teepee of her own."

The priest remained sitting. Don-Ha arose and asked: "Medicine Padre will no more be friend to Indian?"

The priest answered without looking up. He wondered at his answer as the words were uttered. "A woman cannot come between brothers. . . . When are you coming to take Aña from us?"

"Indian no hurry—come soon," said Don-Ha vaguely.

The Padre sat thinking, a humbled man. His eyes turned with a pitiable look to the cell of his many mortifications. "How little compared to my hopes—yet he came to me first. . . ." With all his sentiency the Padre knew hardly a tithe of what it had meant to Don-Ha to come to him first. "The uplifted arm—it is already red," he said, rising and moving slowly to the house of Aña, from which presently a sound of great wailing was heard.

XVI

Don-Ha returned without haste to the Apache camp where he gathered together a dozen young men among his people. Their horses were quickly caught. He led them out into the hills where they made a big circle, constantly under cover from the town. In Don-Ha's thoughts nothing had been missed. This time he was not so lost in the spring planting that he should forget the long testing summer, or the gophers, or the rabbits, or the birds of harvest time. He knew the Medicine Padre would try to keep this matter from the small garrison at Santa Rita to avoid an engagement of arms with the Apaches. He knew that Aña's people would try to take her beyond his reach.

The bucks circled south without loss of time, finally left their horses in the mesquite. Don-Ha gave his direction and they separated to stalk the south road several miles below the village. It was the next day before a mounted party of seven with two extra pack ponies was seen coming from Santa Rita. One was the senorita Aña. She was deeply veiled but not for nuptials. Her father and two brothers and three friends were with her. The dust rose high as their ponies were forced into a lope or trot. They were setting out for the presidio of Janos where soldiers were more plentiful. All of which Don-Ha had foreseen. Had Aña's party been larger, he would have delayed until farther from the Copper Mines, but as it was, he now felt prepared.

As they came very near, he stepped out of the brush

71

to the road, carrying his long rifle in the hollow of his arm as he had seen the trappers do. He raised his left hand signaling them to stop. Under cover the Apaches softly hooted and called to each other on both sides of the trail. Aña screamed as if she had seen the devil. The Mexicans had nothing but their knives and many words. Don-Ha knew them well. They were exhausting their courage with words. He remained silent except for his single sentence when the dust settled:

"I am taking senorita to my teepee."

Finally he said this a second time. The father did not answer but there was low quick talk between him and the brothers. Then Aña with her veil pulled back and a cry for help where there was no help whatsoever, turned her pony back toward the town, two of her brothers following. Hers must have been an old pony with a fondness for village-life, for he started on a gallop, outdistancing the two others.

Six Apaches, unable to restrain a whoop at this climax of the sport, broke out of cover behind and closed in on Aña's mount. Don-Ha facing the three remaining Nakai-yes, saw his companions bring down the prize from the saddle and carry her into the brush, the two brothers not daring to offer resistance. Nor did the three who remained before Don-Ha have the heart to resist the great beast of an Apache with the red arms, and the long rifle before their eyes.

Don-Ha stood silent while they further weakened themselves with violent words, then he said:

"Indian treat good—huh. Pretty soon, senorita no want to come back."

At no time was the rifle raised.

Thus Aña of Santa Rita, crying to Mary, was taken to the teepee of Don-Ha at the Copper Mines, the two squaws already there eyeing her like panthers from the shadows.

XVII

O UTWARDLY an audacious coup, but domestically an
impasse. Don-Ha had still much to do to make his
thought stand among accomplished deeds. A strong man
now was needed to finish what was started in his establishment. His two squaws would not have objected to
a third of their own people; nor would they have objected
to a Mexican girl if permitted to make a slave of her.
Placid and Firefly stood waiting now to know the intention of their lord regarding the newcomer. They were
already of shaded caste because of Don-Ha's notorious
preference for sitting by his night-fires alone. The
grievance now added was not one to be thumped quiet.
They were ready to fight back. Aña sank into the dark-
est corner of the teepee, moaning as if in delirium.

Don-Ha hunched through the flap and stood a moment
for his eyes to find them in the half-dark. Placid came
forward, bare head bowed a little before him.

"What are we to do with this stranger?"

"She is to be one of you—a sister."

He heard the throaty hiss from Firefly, nor did he catch
her by the throat to stop it. He turned and went out.
Presently he saw Firefly emerge and run to her people;
then Placid emerged and went to her father's house.
They returned at nightfall.

Don-Ha sat out as usual that night, listening to all
sounds that came from within. The next day Juan Jose
sent for him.

Juan Jose was fleshy, dissolute and did not balance his

camp gluttony by frequent raids afield. He was a swagger Indian with a drunken gleam in his eye, whether drinking or not. Though past his prime, he had the "hound" look that is part fear and part recklessness—the look of many untried bucks before they have learned to hold their peace. He recognized Don-Ha among the strongest of his young men—and there was in this recognition that which an old bull might know instinctively toward a younger.

There was ceremonial silence.

"Why did you bring this woman here?"

"The Mexican girl many times filled my eyes."

"But we are not at war with the 'cobre' people. It would not have caused so much trouble to capture a woman of a lower village."

"This senorita I have looked upon."

"It will not be well now for us to go in and out of the village of Santa Rita. Our trading will be stopped. We have no mescal to drink."

"The Medicine Padre has not taken his welcome from me."

"You will go in and out of the village as before?"

"In good time I will go again."

"The women of your house are dissatisfied."

"I will deal with them."

"Soldado Fiero is dissatisfied."

"He will send for me to make talk."

"The brothers of the women of your house are dissatisfied."

"Let them come to me."

This was exactly the idea in the mind of Juan Jose. He considered his talk wise and good in that it had brought to this point. Don-Ha returned to his teepee, and was sent for by Soldado Fiero. The talk was much the same, though uglier and without any softening of craft. Don-Ha was given the word as he departed that the affair was by no means finished.

That night he sat outside as usual, and there was only the sound of Aña's wailing from the place of the three women.

Early the next day, Lost Pony, the brother of Placid, came and stood at the ashes of the fire of the night before. Don-Ha gave him greeting. They sat down together. The brother had conferred with Juan Jose, but began the present talk in capitulation of friendship.

"Our arrows have felled the same deer."

"It is so."

"We have cut the same carcass for our fires."

"It is so."

"For years, my brother has been of the same hunt, of the same teaching, of the same feast. Is it not so?"

"It is so."

"When the ninya of my house was ready to take a husband, I informed my friend before all others."

"It is so."

"Long ago when my friend fastened his pony at the door of the teepee of my father, I was much pleased—"

"This I know."

"Now the woman who was of my house and became the woman of your house is dissatisfied."

Don-Ha acquiesced. "And what does my brother consider can be done?"

"The Mexican woman could be sent back."

Without any haste Don-Ha answered: "A woman taken and not kept is a worm. That could not be."

"She could become the property of the tribe—"

"I have taken her to myself for myself."

"She could become a slave to the women already in your house."

"How could that be when I have made her equal?"

The ultimatum was now spoken with the same impassive calm: "Then it is that the shame of this thing is upon my house until death of this—" he pointed to himself, "or that—" he pointed to Don-Ha.

"My brother has spoken?"

"I have spoken."

All of which had been foreseen, even the duel with knives and the prowess of the adversary from the close knowledge of many years.

XVIII

THE combat was ceremoniously arranged for the next day, but neither of the contestants had any part in preparations other than in making themselves ready. Don-Ha's preparations were peculiar. Taking an extra pony with packs, he rode alone in the direction of his cache, pausing in a little canyon, a dozen miles from camp. In a very secluded place where the stream was still, for it is tribal doctrine to avoid noisy water which keeps one from hearing other sounds, he leveled the stones and brought willows and alders weaving a shelter. Then he opened his packs and cached his sacks of food—jerked meat, crushed mesquite beans sweetened with honey, the "banana" of the yucca plant, and certain highly valued packages including a bag of coffee and a jug of mescal from the stores at Santa Rita. He returned at nightfall and did not enter the teepee of the women. Food was brought to him outside and a pallet of deerskins by the fire. There he sat until late and then slept.

Mid-forenoon the next day, he carefully dressed—beaded leggings, red undershirt, deerskin cover shirt, a headdress of turkey red cotton, and after careful pigmenting of his face from his vanity box—went forth to the arena. The village was circled about a trampled space forty feet in diameter. A number of Mexicans of Santa Rita were present, word having gone to the town that Don-Ha's action was not approved of and that the brother of his first wife had undertaken to wipe out the disgrace. This was Juan Jose's way of washing his hands.

78

The careful dressing was perceived to be merely for the walk to the dueling ground, for both principals now disrobed to breech cloth and moccasins and faced each other with left wrists and elbows banded to small oxhide shields, bared butcher knives in the right.

Lost Pony was a big Indian, tall and evenly proportioned. Don-Ha's body was well known in the tribe; it had been regarded studiously by men, women and children for years, since, in fact, his slow prodigious development began to outclass all precedent. What was extraordinarily satisfying to the Apache connoisseur was the way Don-Ha stood upon his feet. These he planted as if fealty were established between them and the earth. From his knees, however, he was seen to poise and sway, perfecting a balance peculiar to himself. The length and thickness of his trunk was of a model unduplicable. Only tradition allowed for anything like it. His head was commensurably huge. Because of these amplifying proportions his unparalleled height was not noticeable until one stood near or saw him tower over the shoulders of tall men. Though Lost Pony's head could have bowed under his chin, the knots of their loin cloths were exactly the same height.

The bodies of both men were smooth, muscles developed for co-ordination rather than show.

Not the slightest appearance of wrath was visible until they began to spar for an opening. Don-Ha's movements were deceptively slow. He rocked sideways as he stepped, weight on the outside of his feet, toes turned in. Both bodies were relaxed, no tension or bunching of muscles. The appearances of speed of movement that go with gathering for a leap or thrust were easily surpassed by the flowing flexible adaptability to the instant need.

The Apache does not waste exertion. He is undone when surprised or caught off his guard; his whole training is in that vigilance that protects him from surprise. The crowd was in a low guttural buzz of delirium. The duelists were fanned with this ferocity of excitement.

It could hardly be said that Don-Ha took the aggressive; rather he was that. He could only be stopped by the other halting to attack or giving himself to close exchange. From the moment of the signal, he pressed his adversary toward the edge of the clearing by advancing indomitably, holding his shield shoulder-high and slightly to the left; his knife lower to the right, blade down as in meeting a man.

Backing his adversary to the cordon of watchers, Lost Pony must either leap to attack or slip aside. He chose the latter and the pursuit began again across the arena. Close to the crowd's edge a second time, the great bearing-down bull of the Mimbrenos struck at the same instant Lost Pony leaped aside. It was not a following, adapting stroke; it was anticipation that included foreknowledge of which way the other would leap, or at least a shrewd accurate guess. The nearby watching braves saw this and murmured. It was the low sophisticated acclaim of expert-players which a champion cares for more than the wildest enthusiasm of those without the eye for fine points.

Lost Pony cleared with a torn abdomen. His head rolled. He saw his death; he felt it. Don-Ha's left leg was wide open below the groin; at the same time he knew something like a small spark in the very core of his brain that augmented his calm. It was this: that Lost Pony not only would not, but could not take the aggressive. Don-Ha's knowledge was entirely within himself; he sensed it in the nature of certainty of his own will power. He held to it and pressed the other a third time across the arena—a bloody walk now. The squaws were mouth-open like coyotes in chorus; they were out of their heads, in the play of lust upon them, old Calico Turkey a seething center.

Broad and hunched, Don-Ha again pressed his adversary across the ring. He seemed distended—a cobra-throated inflation, his shield held far to the left, the knife far to the right, blade down as in meeting a man. The fraction of a second before Lost Pony's back touched the ungiving crowd, Don-Ha launched himself a third time under the uplifted knife of the other, his shield pressed to Lost Pony's breast, hurling him backward.

Now he was kneeling. His right wrist jerked from him and back like a man marking a big figure 7 on the ground.

He regained his feet, wiped his knife between the thumb and forefinger of his left hand, and his hand upon the grass. Behind, on his left shoulder, was a four-inch gash from Lost Pony's last stroke when he was hard pressed and off his feet.

That night Don-Ha sat alone by his fire. His wounds were stiffening. He did not mind the pain, but there was concern about it for another reason. His head bowed over the fire. He was in a concentration deeper than he had ever known before, possibly because of the weakness of his body from loss of blood. In this concentration he regained something in his mind that he had been trying to recapture all afternoon. Now he had it: that sense of invincibility of will power he had known in the combat—power in himself before which Lost Pony had gone weak, unable to take the aggressive. This was good. This was a little grain of good. Years of hard thinking tried out, tested in action and found good. A little bright grain in the core of his brain. It was stronger than death; this he knew.

That night he was visited by Pindah, the elder brother of Firefly and Black Knife, the favorite son of Soldado Fiero. This too had been thought of from the beginning. It had to do with the concern he felt over the stiffening of his wounds. He was glad that it was not Black Knife whom he was to meet tomorrow.

XIX

THE next day Soldado Fiero sat with Juan Jose at the edge of the trampled space. Placid, Firefly and Aña sat with the squaws, and the great crowd ranged round and round. The miners did little work at copper digging that day. Those who had gotten the taste yesterday brought others to the feast.

Pindah was smaller than Lost Pony—swift, small-boned, the color of cobre negro. His body gleamed like a snake that has just sloughed a skin, his eyes scintillated. He was never at rest. Don-Ha watched his movements; he knew them well, as he knew the movements of Firefly's body, and the stealth and suppleness of Black Knife. He knew the consuming hot blood of the breed. The chill and stiffness of his own wounds depressed him, though he had worked his muscles since daybreak to keep them warm. In Pindah he saw more than an enemy of the day. He saw a symbol of the enemy in his own house, in his own tribe.

The signal was given by Juan Jose. Then a murmur went over the crowd, as of some desperate innovation, which Don-Ha had already perceived. Pindah's blade issued from the thumb-side of his hand, as if meeting an animal to butcher head on, not a man upstanding.

This had not been foreseen. It was within the law but an insult deadly as the cut of a whip. The other's strokes would come from below instead of above, also a greater length of stroke was to be avoided. It changed the whole order of defense and attack, but worse than all that, the insult uncentered Don-Ha's volition. His shield lowered over his groin to meet the devilish assumption of attitude, but his mind was filled with a struggle to check the foolish impulse of rage that impelled him to rush in and end the hideous strain—to meet the other with slashing strength instead of his own dominant hasteless calm.

He wrestled with doubt; he was charged with sudden impotence. His mind crowded with reasons why he was not at his best; he felt a conspiracy of the whole tribe against him. A battle in himself, and the lithest surest knife of a knifing race, waiting for him on the trampled grass. Don-Ha held back, surveying the adversary a moment longer.

His eye moved to Juan Jose and he met no friend in that evasive glitter. Firefly's face had a forked look; even Placid burned to see Pindah wipe out with his knife the shame which her brother had failed to atone; squaws everywhere athirst for the blood of one who dared to bring in a foreigner and not for slavery. The younger men were not with him; they had looked also upon senoritas, but without daring to bring their desires to action; Half-Foot, Black-Knife, Soldado Fiero—he felt himself caught in a triangular trap of their hatred. The massed Mimbreno thought against him was like an impact upon his brow.

Thus Don-Ha met the great moment of loneliness, which forces a man to turn in to himself. A divided self is no self. He was forced likewise to find that hard bright grain of his own volition that he had become aware of yesterday. Without this mastery he could not hope to master another. This mastery could only be found in stillness, never in the din and turmoil of a mind charged with doubt and hate. The sneering face of Pindah had to be shut from his eyes.

Thus he hesitated at the edge of the trampled space— to find his own stillness, and in that moment the crowd fell upon his cowardice with a great yell of relief, for the secret of every Apache heart was placated. The great young bull of Juan Jose's Mimbrenos was not as yesterday; today he was a calf at heart. Now Don-Ha stepped cautiously forward, knowing the unrestrained jeers of his own people in whom cruelty is a bottomless pit.

He sparred defensively; caution cramped his limbs. Already a voice cried, "Pindah," as if designating the victor. Another instant he leaped back to avoid a viper thrust almost invisibly swift from the other's hip. His mind was clearing; still he played for time, coping with tribal hate as he had not known it before, because it was centered now upon himself.

Then came the instant when those close about saw him fix his eyes upon Pindah as if seeing clearly for the first time. He had caught his own thought; defense below, attack above. His head lowered. His crouched body moved forward; his knees became alive again; he thudded the earth with his feet as if regaining contact; his body loosened and balanced again upon his knees. Pindah refused to give; the shields crashed. The weight of the greater man was not stopped.

The bull was back to the ring, his legs tramping in rhythm. To stand before him now was to check an all but irresistible rhythmic advance. Don-Ha's limbs were stating the terms of the whole man. These terms were cold, ultimate, conclusive. A moment before he had not been dealing with one man merely, but with the will of his house, with the will of his tribe, with the combined resistance of a whole people against granting his intrinsic supremacy, as well as a host of responsive doubts and fears in himself. Now he could concentrate on the work before him. The battle had focalized to one foe, a sinister flash of speed and guile, not to be taken lightly.

Pindah offered his bare back to the knife, and in a spinning sweep struck under the shield, but Don-Ha's body was not there. He was moved by no strategy of another; he was carrying out his own. Defense below—attack above. Pindah tripped to stretch him out in attack, but Don-Ha merely pressed a step forward. Every step, every second, was nearer the end. He had only to do this one thing to the end, not to be deluded with an instant's relaxation, an instant's glow of advantage, or instant's quailing with the fight against him.

He pressed Pindah to the crowd. He read the stroke as it came. His shield shot to the left, crashing the wrist of Pindah's knife hand. From above, his right drove at Pindah's throat.

It was not enough. Pindah's head miraculously remained upstanding on his shoulders—a wide descending curtain of blood sheeting his breast—eyes looking out at him, in which the end was written, but also a prayer, an offer of eternal allegiance to Gods of the Shadow, if he might be permitted to kill his enemy at the moment of death. Eyes of severed look and sorcerer's prayer.

Thus standing, Pindah's left hand whipped over to take the knife from the useless right, and he flung forward, striking like a bob-cat in the leap. Don-Ha met the blow with a twisting hook of the shield that released the knife itself. As yesterday, he knelt to finish the day.

Looking up, he heard Juan Jose laugh; then he heard the cries, the wild pandemonium, and knew that it had been going on all the time, though he had worked in silence. The rage was gone from him. The law had cut it clean.

His right forearm was sheeted with blood, but that was Pindah's, not his own. The blood upon his knife was not his own. He remembered the words of the Padre, and raised the dripping arm above his people. He moved to the place his squaws had sat. Aña alone was there, eyes empty as a sitting corpse, the red shirt at her knees. He picked it up and drew it over his right shoulder—thrusting one arm through. As his hand appeared, a voice sounded:

"La-choy Ko-kun-noste!"

The name Don-Ha and Dasoda-hae began to be forgotten from that moment, his new name being established on every lip.

"La-choy Ko-kun-noste—Red Sleeve!"

XX

Apache law is simple and clean cut: it works with no uncertain stroke. He had earned Aña beyond any gainsaying of his house or of his tribe. He was now beyond question in the flaccid conjurings of Juan Jose, even in the angry and grief-whipped brain of Soldado Fiero himself. No matter what these two thought on their own account; the matter was settled.

Red Sleeve had risen instead of fallen. He had bitten off a big piece, swallowed it, digested it, made it contribute to his strength. He had chosen a name and made it stand. Their own likes and dislikes were their own affair. There are no conspiracies against the law of the tribe. Red Sleeve was a man among men, a man among themselves, chiefs of men.

As for himself, torn and spent, there was nevertheless the beginnings of new life in body and brain. Because it had been earned, he was not light-headed. One may be light-headed or inflated over sudden good fortune when it is stolen or falls his way by chance, but when one earns a thing in the long slow way of thoughts carried out, he has also earned the strength and balance to carry that thing in the form of knowledge and authority.

He was at peace rather than exultant; his peace was of the nature of solid calm which he felt in his throat and chest and loins. He had not to raise his voice because others listened better; they came closer and bowed to hear. He had to say less because they gave him attention.

He had no force to waste on people, for by law the lesser obeys the greater. The man who speaks loudly or emphasizes with blows has not earned his place, even if he occupies the place of a leader. He has stolen it or it has fallen his way by chance. Sooner or later he will lose it and sink back where he belongs.

Placid bound his wounds. Cool hands are good for this. He did not despise her now, for he had paid her back for her trick of making him take a glowworm to his nest. Their score was settled. The glowworm herself ran to wait on him, her narrow face queer as if an ashen hand had smeared it; queer, too, in the question it carried. A question not to father or brother, squaw or medicine man—a question no one could answer but herself. It had to be lived out, and the manner of living was different from ever before—an altogether new place, position, attitude to life and tribe. She had watched her brother pay for questioning her lord. She had watched Placid's brother pay.

Red Sleeve regarded her. He did not feel like telling her where she belonged; it was not necessary. He was lord, no less. He watched her without seeming to look, but she knew his eyes were on her as never before, and her head bowed, though she did not know.

Law is simple and clean cut; it works, when it works at all in the Apache camp, with no uncertain stroke. It had cut many people in this stroke; Placid and her family, Firefly and hers; it had performed upon every member of the tribe. The unanimous hate reared against him had been cut like a bladder. It was now as a sickness difficult to remember. He had conquered that sickness.

The law of the knife had cut him free from a questionable mediocrity and made his every word and movement significant. More, it had made him a law unto himself. All he had to do was to maintain his place. It had cut Firefly free from all she had fancied herself. That was why her whole body and face was curved into a question.

He chose her now to work upon. His word was for her to see that Aña was washed and clothed. She dove into the teepee. Well enough, so far. He waited coolly enough, as he lay resting. He could have told Placid to get the horses, but he was not working upon her now. Firefly was gone long in the teepee. He listened for sounds from within, but there were none. She came out, saying Aña was ready.

"Two saddle horses, one pack horse," he said, designating which horses. Again she ran to obey. This was well. He now permitted Placid to prepare further packs, which was done while the horses were being brought. When they were ready, he spoke again, a demand that Aña be led out. Without questioning each other, the two squaws hurried to obey. This was well and as he intended. Aña was led forth between them—fringed, beaded, combed and with the look of the church in her eyes—

Prayer to the Virgin in her eyes.

She mounted. Red Sleeve felt the eyes of the tribe upon him. Crowded faces in the teepee flaps—like shining points in the dark. Let eyeballs continue to fill. He was walking in history this day, as one fording a deep river. The pack animal was led up, its string in Aña's hand. That was good.

He was bleeding. His body was wet and hot under loin cloth and breech and shirt. This could be endured.

"Raise separate teepee there—" he designated the place, "—ready when I myself return."

He led the way toward the sequestered canyon without looking back.

XXI

N<small>A-TSE-KES.</small>

The Apache verb to think. It means somewhat more than the word as ordinarily used. It means to have one subject at a time, to the exclusion of all others, and to turn it over again and again in the mind. To cover this meaning, the word *meditate* is better.

To have a subject and to turn it over again and again in the mind—that is na-tse-kes. It is an Apache mental process, or the word would not be of such significance in the tribe, but as an art it was developed by Red Sleeve more than any other. This was now perceived without reservation among all Mimbrenos.

A chief among men is one who does the thinking for other men. His brain is like an invisible magnet sweeping over iron filings. Other men cannot think where he is; their thoughts fall away before his more powerful thoughts; their efforts to think are swept in to feed his. Sometimes they fall asleep where he is, or nod continually, or rise and go away; others find it unnecessary to think where he is, and this is a relief to many.

Thus a leader is made.

The Apache is a chief by his own will; by his own assumptions first, then by making good on them. It is not enough to have thoughts; thoughts must be carried out. Apaches are not easily swept in by an assumption of leadership. They are proud of being individuals. Having no flocks or barns or fields, they have nothing to lose, nothing to bind them together for mutual protection.

They are independent, on their own, a stiff-necked congregation. A man in their midst must be powerful to gain authority in the first place; after that he is required constantly to demonstrate his authority, to prove himself over and over again.

A man who is never allowed for a moment the fatuous sense of arrival, neither in his own mind nor among his own people; never permitted to rest, but continually forced to surpass himself—such a man accumulates prodigious growth. In any other tribe Red Sleeve would have been an arrived man at thirty-five. Among the Pimas or Opatas he would have appeared as a traditional giant, a heaven-born, but among his own unimpressionable people, he was merely the most gazed upon, the most discussed.

Soldado Fiero was indisputably the chief of the Warm Springs Apaches and Juan Jose still ostensibly leader of the Copper Mine people, though neither in a crisis would have been looked to now as Red Sleeve. The crisis had not yet arrived, although the latter practiced in his thoughts constantly the words and ways of leadership.

As the trail of an enemy or friend is followed studiously, often on hands and knees, the trails of Red Sleeve's thinkings were now followed by other men, his actions studied and traced back to the thoughts that instigated them.

To discover Red Sleeve's full meaning in an action, and the processes that brought it about, became a sitting game well approved.

Over and over again, that moment in which he was hated more than any other—the moment in which he hesitated before leaving the edge of the ring with Pindah

waiting jeeringly in the center—was discussed around
many Apache fires. It was seen that just there he had
shown the highest stroke of his genius, for he had waited
to find himself, to find his thought, under strange and
altered conditions.

The Apache does not believe in losing his life. The
warpath to him is the greatest of sports, as well as being
the easiest way of making a living, but to die on the warpath is a calamity unmitigated. He does not care reck-
lessly to shine for others' eyes so much as to enjoy the
feasts of victory after the skirmish is over. In fact, there
is no incentive to be reckless, for it is not considered
heroic. Foolhardiness is just what the word implies. Life
here is heaven enough; the happy hunting grounds of the
Apache are not far aloft in remote ethers, but earthbound,
as close as possible. There is only one excuse for expos-
ing oneself to the enemy, or dying for other Apaches,
and that is when one has already received a death wound.
In that case the Apache accepts heroism as a sad second
choice.

All of which made significant the pausing of Red
Sleeve before joining battle with the hot-blooded Pindah.
That lowest moment became the highest. Likewise every
phase of his combat with Lost Pony was considered; and
over and over again his carrying out the solitary coup
among the trappers, and his taking captive the senorita
and making his house and his tribe adjust to suit his own
pleasure.

Absolute lordship in his own wickiup had been accomplished. This was not easily acquired. Many Apaches
had the name of being unspotted warriors afield who were
not unreservedly esteemed among squaws in general, nor

eagerly served and waited upon around their private fires.

But in one thing the trail of Red Sleeve's thoughts was not followed so readily. Sitting alone by the fire was understood and admired, but not the bringing of his pallet to his solitary fire. Placid had not broken this strange habit, nor Firefly, about whom there was more masculine curiosity than any other young squaw among the Mimbrenos. Firefly's name, out of Red Sleeve's hearing, was pivotal no less, with that of unattainable experience. Yet Firefly had not held Red Sleeve from his wooings of the solitary night.

It was believed, however, that Aña of Santa Rita would change all this; though there were a few, among them Calico Turkey, who stood back of the throne of Ne-pot-on-je, medicine chief of all Mimbrenos, who saw deeper into the weave of the Red Sleeve fabric and expressed doubt.

XXII

Red Sleeve returned with Aña at midforenoon on the twelfth day. The separate teepee was prepared and Aña entered to find all that was needed in readiness there. She emerged presently, having apparently no thought of entering upon her life of labor this day. Meanwhile Red Sleeve had three other ponies brought and with Aña and a young Apache called Delgadito (the Slender) set out for Santa Rita del Cobre, but paused at the edge of the village from which another party was now emerging—Padre Font and two women.

Aña and Delgadito came to a pause but within hearing; the two followers of the Padre also lingered behind him a short distance. The other two came together with hands extended.

"Fumaso tobaho?" said Red Sleeve.

"Yes, Don-Ha," Father Font said, bringing forth tobacco and papers.

"No call Don-Ha any more—"

"What shall I say?"

The other pointed to the exposed sleeve of turkey red, repeating the Indian name, which the other understood.

"So that is it," the priest said. "Mangus Colorado."

"Huh—how you say again?"

"Mangus Colorado."

"Mangus Colorado," the Apache repeated, the tone scarcely audible, for one does not speak his own name aloud.

"That is it."

"Huh—smoke good. No cafe aqui—" a trace of a smile with this.

"Aqui, no. In the village—"

"Some time come. Not now."

They sat and smoked.

"Take senorita back to her people—huh?"

"But Don-Ha, my friend—Mangus Colorado—you must not ask that! She would have a bitter time—worse than death."

The Indian's face was impassive. He appeared considering deeply.

"Mexican people no want senorita back?" he finally said.

"No—not now. You must understand what you have done!"

"Ask woman what *she* want."

The priest raised his eyes to Ana. She came forward to him.

"Aña, do you want to come back to the village—to your people?"

"No, Padre."

"You will stay with this man? Glad to stay?"

"Yes."

"That is well. My friend played with me," the priest added, greatly relieved.

Red Sleeve faintly smiled. "Tell him," he said to Aña.

"I have teepee by myself. I am treated very well."

"I am glad, Aña. I am glad for you, too, my friend."

"You say—all people say—Mexican girl no go back to her people after she have Indian baby. Not so. She no go back now. One-half moon—no baby."

"I see. It is quite as you say. I hope it will continue

so. Would you permit Aña's mother to see her for a moment? She asked to come with me."

Red Sleeve waved his hand broadly, signifying that he did not prevent the mother from looking.

"But close—in her arms?"

"Nah—no good—make sick. She Indian woman now."

He never used the name Aña. His name for her always brought a hush-gesture from the Padre, and color to the old face. The two parties separated as before, with Delgadito a witness of the ceremony. A man of authority permits others to dilate upon his doings.

That night Red Sleeve sat by his fire alone as usual. Placid came to replenish the fire from time to time. Firefly brought tobacco and water. The loose tongues of two teepees licked lightly in the breeze. Their lord sat late, and finally called for his deerskin pallet. He sat upon it, drew his blankets about him and presently leaned back. An inaudible murmur moved among the teepees, reaching even the central medicine lodge of the Mimbrenos.

"Red Sleeve become big chief," said Ne-pot-on-je. "Red Sleeve plenty tall man—look over heads of tall men. Red Sleeve thoughts also very tall."

Calico Turkey gave him the fox laugh. "Squaws' heads not so tall," she said.

"Red Sleeve soon become big chief," repeated the Bear Watcher. "Come day not far off Red Sleeve walk among Coyoteros. Among Chihuicahui men, among Mescalero men—hold head very high—"

"Red Sleeve pretty soon become big chief not because his thoughts go over head of tall men—because thoughts go over low head of many squaw," said Wano-boono. "Red Sleeve like himself better than pretty new squaw."

XXIII

Soldado Fiero had heard Juan Jose laugh. That was
not good. The Apache, though an enemy to other people, is slow to quarrel in his own tribe. The two Mimbreno camps under Juan Jose and Soldado Fiero had sep-
arately operated for many years, but were only familiarly
at odds with each other; a campaign against a common
enemy would have united them in indissoluble fraternity.
Still the copper camp of Mexicans at Santa Rita was a
constant and growing irritation between them, and the
laugh of Juan Jose at the moment of Red Sleeve's kneeling
to finish Pindah did not help.

Red Sleeve sat long and often silently at the central
fires of both parties. There was in him that which the
Medicine Padre either recognized or implanted from the
beginning, with his talk about a bridge, a unifying principle. The Padre had hoped this bridge would become
serviceable between the Mexicans of Santa Rita and the
Apache people, but that was more than any one man
could bring about. There were too many others to undo
the work of one man. Miners were constantly increasing;
the Apaches more and more restless and dissatisfied at
this noisy and lumbering host occupying the very center
of their habitat, digging away at the very foundation
of their council rocks.

Long dusky conductas stretched out continually between the Copper Mines and the Pass into Chihuahua
and Durango to the southeast, and from the Copper

Mines to Sonora in the southwest. From their observation peaks, the Apache watched these attenuated traffic lines with spidery patience, but eyes that preyed already, eyes that feasted on thoughts of the kill.

However, a semblance of a bridge was at least operative between the two Apache camps. Red Sleeve strung his invisible girders back and forth by his own comings and goings. It is possible that in foreseeing his own leadership, he did not wish to be leader over a mere half of the Mimbrenos. Also he had another small thought—now complete and ready to carry out.

That winter's take of furs of the Pattie party was well tanned by this time and converted into provisions and more enduring properties, but one day Red Sleeve went alone to the old cache. So much time had elapsed that the Mimbrenos had put away the idea of several rifles as a part of the young warrior's booty. It was now supposed that there had been but one rifle, the same which Red Sleeve carried with distinguishing grace. This day he made his way back to the Warm Springs instead of his own place, and sat down with a firing-piece across his knees, which no one observed to be other than the one he usually carried. Black Knife appeared and also sat down. Tobacco was brought and a cloud blown between them.

"Lessons learned together are not quickly forgotten," said Red Sleeve.

Black Knife grunted.

"At the time I myself began to remember, there were no Mexicans here—nor was there a Mexican name for this Indian, nor one for his friend."

Black Knife nodded. Santa Rita already had begun to put Black Knife into Spanish—"Cuchillo Negro," a sign of his importance as a man set apart. By no means was this name spoken to the degree that "Mangus Colorado" was now spoken, but at least it was designated.

"Arrows are good and easily obtained," said Red Sleeve. "Arrows are silent and not to be discarded. My friend sends his arrows more truly than most of our people."

The son of Soldado Fiero let that pass between friends.

"Bullets for pesh-e-gar are not easily obtained. There is no one among our people to fashion the same from black iron and the fire."

Red Sleeve furthermore explained that the gray black seeds which made a great noise upon application of the spark could not be planted in the ground like other seeds which bring forth their kind—that moisture was not good for these struck-by-lightning seeds. Moisture, in fact, was assiduously to be avoided in all fire-stick dealings. He then added:

"Pesh-e-gar which I hold in my hands is good. It has not lain in water and dirt. It is straight and carries true. I have tried it before bringing it to my friend—"

Black Knife's beady eyes glittered, as he held out his hands.

"Lessons learned together are well learned and long remembered," he said.

A thing greatly discussed afterward had been done. Red Sleeve had not curried favor with Juan Jose by a gift beyond price, nor angered Juan Jose by bestowal to Soldado Fiero. In either case he would have widened the rift between the two camps. In binding Black Knife to him in friendship, he bound the camps together and washed out any lingering personal enmity for the slaying of Pindah. Red Sleeve had little fear of Black Knife as a personal rival, for the son of Soldado Fiero lacked the power of putting two and two together, and the coolness necessary to sit long over his thoughts.

XXIV

O ne day Mimbreno scouts reported that in one of the conductas from Sonora via Janos were two strange wagons, each carrying thick iron reeds, bigger at the closed end than the open end, of the length of a boy and the thickness of a jug of mescal . . .

It was Juan Jose's weakness in the beginning. This was freely granted. Many years had passed, but it was by no means forgotten that Juan Jose had let in the Mexican miners in the first place, and life now was not pure. The children of the Apaches of the old camp were banefully smart in Mexican ways, to the marked dislike of their elders. More miners were coming and their conductas into Mexico were longer and better armed and more constantly coming and going.

No, Juan Jose was not given to great ranging journeys as aforetime. He was a haunch-sitter, placated with presents. When he went out it was like a fat squaw who cannot swim, keeping in shallow water close to the bank. But Soldado Fiero took his people out, months at a time. His people were more truly Apache. They were sullen, hard, swift. They brought home the horses, and when the Mexicans inquired, made no answer, such questions being beneath them.

Once when Soldado Fiero was coming back from Sonora with a drove of horses and Mexican beef on the hoof, running their stock along an arroyo two days' journey from the Copper Mines, soldiers from the barracks at Janos were seen approaching at a distance. They planted a flag of white. Soldado Fiero and his staff of braves could have scattered up among the timber, but the scouts had reported upon the number of the soldiers. It was not overpowering; moreover Soldado Fiero was in no mood to be delayed now, well within his own hunting ground, only two days away from the feasts of homecoming. He halted, however, and signified his readiness for parley.

The Mexican officer said he had news of cattle and horses stolen from the lower villages, and it was necessary for him to corral the present booty of the Apaches until he proved that these had been properly obtained.

It was told long afterward around Apache fires how Soldado Fiero raised himself in the saddle sidewise, with a movement not to be misinterpreted by the Mexicans, also a small gesture of the hand to his own braves which they understood electrically, and began at once turning the stock up toward the hills. Soldado Fiero with a sneering smile conveyed his answer to the effect that if the Mexicans would kindly come higher they would stand a better chance of getting the stock for the Janos corrals.

Now the cattle and horses were in flight on rising trails, the bucks in full cry after them. Soldado turned his back and heeled his mount to follow, but a shot from behind rocked him in the saddle. His braves closed about him, as they lashed their ponies up toward the rim-rocks.

Presently it was seen that the Mexicans were following. Soldado Fiero was apprised of this, and though desperately wounded, ordered his men to continue higher, toward a sparse growth of timber, strewn with great boulders. Reaching there, he sent all saddle beasts farther on with the boys of the party and lay with the rest in wait. The Mexicans climbed into the ambush and met a sudden deadly rain of arrows released by Apaches inflamed by the sight of the blood of their chief. The men from Janos fell back, leaving their wounded behind.

These the Apaches finished in a fashion more merciful than usual, being pressed for time to get Soldado Fiero to the big medicine lodge at the home camp. The main party was left to round up the horses and cattle, and litter-bearers under escort kept going for twenty straight hours. Already the news was five hours old at the Copper Mines and Warm Springs, a fleet runner having made a non-stop passage.

A great wailing din, together with sounds of thudding feet, issued from the medicine lodge as the litter of Soldado was carried in before dawn. Ne-pot-on-je, the stolid old sorcerer of the Mimbrenos, did not rise but watched from a corner. Calico Turkey sat near him; neither did she rise, but the medicine men of lesser esteem gathered closely about, were careful not to shut off the view of the litter from the elders.

Ne-pot-on-je from where he sat merely glanced casually into the contorted face of the fallen leader, fighting for life. His eyes then fixed upon the thin darkness, vague with firelight, a foot above Soldado's forehead, and finally fixed beyond the head of the pallet, two hands' breadth from Soldado's crown. At last Ne-pot-on-je spoke, and Red Sleeve standing just outside heard the words:

"Black bird of death perch on Soldado Fiero's chest. Must fly off quick or war chief soon be dead."

The other medicine men took their cue from this and started making passes and violent sneering gestures at the

black presence indicated by Ne-pot-on-je. Weird chant-
ing and praying sounded outside. Hoddentin, the yellow
flour of the swamp rush, was scattered thickly about
the lodge.

During the next four hours the battle waged. The
vitality of the chieftain was powerfully integrated in his
flesh. If there was any advantage in silence for his life
or death crisis, it was not granted to him. Perhaps in the
fury of organic disintegration, he did not hear the outer
din; rawhide drums in muffled thunder and pebbled
gourds rattling beside them. The ululation reached its
ictus, then died down.

The fangs of the death vampire had sunk too deep to
be frightened away. The moment had come when the
spirit of Soldado Fiero could no longer stay within his
body.

A stench filled the place.

Ne-pot-on-je looked at Calico Turkey; then stared up
into the peak of the lodge, his eyes widely distended in
listening. Calico Turkey also cocked her head in intense
listening attitude. Finally Ne-pot-on-je spoke:

"Soldado Fiero climb out, leave body to black bird.
Black bird stay here—now feed inside. Soldado gone—
take long sleep outside. Before he go, Soldado Fiero
speak to Ne-pot-on-je from top of lodge."

Calico Turkey rasped her throat.

"Soldado Fiero speak to Wano-boono also," gravely cor-
rected the Bear Watcher. "Leave message for all Mimbreno people!"

The rawhide drums outside sounded a different note;
all within reach of the sound gathered about the medicine lodge.

"Free from the body, the spirit is without pain," Ne-pot-on-je began, and the people fell into deep silence. "Free from the body, the spirit see more clearly. Soldado Fiero say Copper Mine Indian get fat. Say Copper Mine Indian sleep too much. Lance fall from hand. Say Warm Springs Indian and Copper Mine Indian all one— take warpath together. Drive out Santa Rita Nakai-yi— Janos Nakai-yi—"

Ne-pot-on-je paused to pick up a nip of trampled dust between his fingers and place it on the palm of his hand.

"Soldado Fiero say all Mimbreno Indian drive out all Nakai-yes like that—" he exploded the little dust pile with a puff from his lips.

Red Sleeve considered that Soldado Fiero did not have to die to say that. Evidently Ne-pot-on-je could think of nothing more. "Soldado Fiero get pretty sleepy 'bout that time," he added, and Calico Turkey glared at her consort for his anticlimax.

XXV

Black Knife, whose name had now taken its Spanish form of Cuchillo Negro, counselled an immediate laying siege to Santa Rita, but Juan Jose declared that direct warfare would cost too many men, and that it would bring more soldiers from the garrison at Janos, which of late had been greatly increased. Cuchillo Negro could see only more delay in this, and disgustedly set out again for Sonora to avenge the death of his father. He took with him over a hundred Warm Springs Apaches.

Santa Rita was not formally closed to the Mimbrenos, but few felt free to enter, in the light of recent affairs. Several days later, a party of boys venturing too close to the mining camp were fired upon by the soldiers. Three of the boys fell, the rest running away. From their distant observation points soon afterward the Apaches saw the Mexicans come out to the spot where the three boys lay in the sun. The bodies were not taken away, however, nor were they covered. When the Apaches crept up to them after nightfall, they were found to be scalped.

The next day the Medicine Padre came out under truce, carrying his cross. He asked for "Mangus Colorado," who went to meet him, conducting him to the teepee of Juan Jose. The Padre told of his great grief that these things had happened. He begged Mangus Colorado on the strength of their old friendship to understand that all Mexicans in Santa Rita were not like those who had done this thing; that there was a decided difference in feeling between Sonora Mexicans and Chihuahua Mexicans; that

Sonora was now offering money for Apache scalps; and some of the leaders of the mining interests favored doing the same. Chihuahua, he declared, was not in this terrible business. Chihuahua still believed in feeding the Indian and keeping the Indian friend. If time could be given, the Padre believed he could make the people of Santa Rita undivided in their determination to keep peace with the Indian and make reparation for the killing and scalping of the Indian boys. He asked for time. Furthermore, he declared that the soldiers who went out to stop Soldado Fiero and examine the horses and cattle had not meant to fire upon the Apaches; that this was the work of one soldier who was punished afterward.

The Apaches did not miss that the Padre, in all this talk, looked only to Red Sleeve. Though they understood little or nothing, they listened in grave silence. After discussion, Juan Jose chose Red Sleeve to interpret the Mimbreno side. The latter was well aware of the cold ugliness and insolent distrust back of the grave demeanor of his people; also he knew that the only two points of interest to the Mimbrenos were reparation for the killing and scalping of three Indian boys, and the kind of punishment that had been inflicted upon the soldier who shot Soldado Fiero. Red Sleeve finally spoke:

"Long ago, Copper Mine Indian move over to make place for Mexican miner in his own mountains," he began. "Mexican miner come in, bring wife and senorita, bring firewater and guns. More Mexican miners come in. Indian crowd over some more and see miner come and go in his place. Long ago, Mimbreno Indian all one camp. After Mexican miner come in, Mimbreno Indian two camps. Indian people not free and happy any more.

"One day Mimbreno chief come home with cattle and horses. Mexican soldier shoot and kill Indian chief. . . . One day Apache boy go near village of Santa Rita. Mexican soldiers shoot and kill Apache boy. Come out and take scalp.

"This day Medicine Padre come—long for peace. Medicine Padre make true talk. Friends know when talk is good. Word of Medicine Padre mean much to Mimbreno Indian, but Mexican people promise many thing; no keep word. Friendship between two men is not same as friendship between two peoples. Bad time come for all Mimbreno; bad time come for Mexican. Time of end very near. Mimbreno now want to know what punishment was given to Mexican soldier who shoot and kill Indian chief."

"He was sent to the prison for soldiers at Janos," said Father Font eagerly.

All Mimbreno faces carried the sinister curve of derision when this answer was conveyed. Red Sleeve turned again to the Padre:

"The leader of my people want to know more what Mexican people mean to pay for killing and taking scalp of Apache boy."

"That is a matter not settled yet," said Father Font. "That I will take up with my people as soon as I return."

His face was very white and weary. He now realized the weakness of his position, yet his eyes lingered on Red Sleeve with the unmistakable affection of a master toward an old disciple. He searched the deep-set glistening eyes for mercy. His own haggard look deepened. He may have remembered that day when Red Sleeve had come with word that he was taking Aña to his teepee. Yet to his eyes Mangus Colorado was now a different man, his eyes deeper, brighter; his voice deeper, calmer. The Padre took courage and called upon the Spirit that had never failed to move the fitful hearts of the Mexican people.

". . . Believe in us of Chihuahua a little longer! By my word, which has never been broken to you, I promise to give my life if necessary to bring this peace. I come to ask you to bear with me, without carrying on war, until I can bring about a concerted purpose in Santa Rita. If the decision of my people is against Indian friendship, I myself will come and tell you. If there can be organized an undivided determination for peace in Santa Rita, I myself will bring the terms. In the meantime, truce between us—"

Low gutturals of scorn and detestation filled the air. The fact of imprisonment in Janos for the Mexican soldier was foolishly aside the mark. Apache law decreed that the soldier belonged to the Apache for punishment. As for the killing of Apache boys, there was only one lawful answer for that. The Medicine Padre had not brought the answer, nor would the Copper Mine Apache wait much longer. Red Sleeve himself was altogether unmoved by the Padre's appeal. He agreed with Juan Jose, however, in giving the Padre a chance to go and come again with decisive word.

XXVI

Apache signal smokes from a hunting band ranging in high country to the north relayed the information that a big party of whites was on the way toward the Copper Mines. This was during one of the waiting days before the second hearing from Father Font. Juan Jose sent braves to close in and report in detail upon the outfit of strangers.

No movement of the white party was missed thereafter. They numbered fifteen and were coming down through the timber range of the Pinos Altos, heavily armed, with five pack mules. They neither hurried nor paused for long. They kept well together and were without fear or idea of concealment.

Red Sleeve himself watched them for a whole day. He heard their voices and laughter. They made him think of Chawn-clizzay and his three and the boy. Watching them made him restless and started the old burning at the pit of his stomach. The Mexicans never caused this, nor started thoughts that were without conclusion or purpose. The Spaniards never made him feel this way.

These whom he now watched were laughing men; if it was not one who laughed, it was another. They fought, too; there was first a sudden snarling like a bear and cougar in the same thicket; then two tall men stood up close and pounded each other with blows of the hand, containing neither knife nor rock. All the others gathered close around, examining each blow, sometimes making signs of blows but in the air only. Then one of the whites fell, and there was a great roar of relief, also laughter, then everyone said their favorite words.

Those words warmed Red Sleeve. It was not friendliness he felt toward the whites; it was as if he knew something about them that could not be spoken; something that other Indians did not know; that had to do with things not precisely remembered or not yet come to fruit in deeds. Many winters had passed since that full moon and more of watching the other party under old Goatface whom the Mexicans called "Senor Pat-tee," but his thinking about them had continued; the way they played, the way they laughed, their terrible anger coming down the mountain the second time, but especially the way they used the rifle. Yes, he had thought very well of them, and of these white men too, he thought well. The more he despised the Mexicans, and the Spaniards behind them, the more he thought well of whites, but there was in his thinking a nameless disturbance.

The chief of these whites was not like Chawn-clizzay. All the same tall, but not old. He laughed loudest. He spoke the names of all others and slapped their shoulders. Also he lifted his leg to slap that. Yet he was not like a leader who knows himself in himself and contains his followers without fear. He had the hound look like Juan Jose.

Finally the whites strode down upon Santa Rita del Cobre, where no Apache now could follow. Their voices were heard that day and into night. They were feasting. The senoritas would be snatched from their dancing; lamps of the shops burned long after day was ended. Red Sleeve watched and listened at a distance.

Feasting was good, when one has covered much country. Drinking was good when one has traveled long with springs far apart, but feasting and drinking every day was not good. One grew like the duck on the bank, too heavy to take wing. But soon the lights of Santa Rita would be Indian fires again, and the senoritas would be tramping the dust to Janos and beyond. Red Sleeve picked up a nip of dust between his fingers, thinking of Ne-pot-on-je's words. Toward the end of the third day, the strangers not having departed, the Medicine Padre was seen coming with his cross and his flag of white; also at this time word was brought in that another party of whites was coming down through the passes of the mountains.

"I bring glad tidings," said the Medicine Padre, raising his hands above them. "God has breathed upon the work I was sent to do. The policy of Chihuahua is favored above that of the party of Sonora, and I am sent to invite you and your women and children to a great feast tomorrow, at which your head men and the head men of the miners may speak in amity together. There are also in our midst at this time, white men from the far north and east who will hear the words spoken and be witness to the treaty between us!"

Juan Jose's vanity was touched. His eyes also gleamed at the thought of high celebration tomorrow after dragging home-brew days. Red Sleeve asked what reparation had been determined upon for the death of the Indian boys.

"All that will be answered tomorrow," said the Padre, who wrung his hand and departed.

"Mexican words no pay for dead Apache boy," muttered Juan Jose. "Mexican cobre no pay. Mexican white iron—yellow iron no pay. Mexican boy—how many—pay for dead Apache boy?"

XXVII

THAT night Red Sleeve sat long by his fire. The pit of his stomach burned steadily; his thoughts were fitful and without peace. Once and for all, the Medicine Padre would not lie; that was established. Yet Red Sleeve liked not the conclusion of affairs in Santa Rita with white strangers present. His sole idea of justice was Apache justice. Justice demanded the like; otherwise justice sickened and men with it, all becoming confused among men. Mexican boys only would pay for Apache boys, though Red Sleeve knew it was not like the Mexicans to supply boys for this. Medicine Padre would say two wrongs do not make a right, which was of course untrue, but the Padre believed it, having said the same many times. Moreover, the Padre would say, "What boys can we choose? We do not keep boys for that purpose. Parents do not make boys for that purpose in Mexican village."

He could only conclude that the work of the Medicine Padre had been done particularly well this time; that this was no ordinary occasion and Santa Rita was making a great and final stand for peace. Not that Mimbreno wanted peace, with miners coming and going in Mimbreno country. The Mimbreno was tired of that confusion of all peace. He wanted his land again, to live his own life again. Peace on any terms was not desirable, yet Apache must listen to Medicine Padre once more.

Sleep did not come. Fire signals showed that night carrying word that the second party of white men, of equal number to the first, was within two days' jornada from the Copper Mines. This was not good. Mimbreno country was broken in like teepee with a hole in the back as well as the front.

XXVIII

THE NEXT dawn saw great preparation in the Apache camp and also among the squaws and children at the Warm Springs hangout, Soldado Fiero and his warriors still away on a raid. A dawn of much hoddentin sprinkling.

Fiesta; in all Mimbreno memory no day like this. First there would be eating and drinking, then the Mexicans would speak. Finally the Mimbreno, who knew his own mind, would speak; without haste he would put his thoughts into words, when eating and drinking were well finished.

Squaws put on what they had of beads and fringed leather and cloth. Not a cloud; the day promised hot, but one could not leave behind any adornment on a day like this. Papooses were swathed and sewed into their upright cradles for the day; others were taken by the hand, still others, lively and attentive, were herded within hearing like young quail.

Aña by her own choice was not to go. She did not wish to meet her own people and be whispered about and laughed at in the village. Placid and Firefly looked upon her, darkly triumphant.

Braves peered into fragments of glass and plucked hairs from their faces, painting the skin carefully with ochre and vermillion. They caught and mounted their brightest ponies; squaws and children walking in the dust behind them. All bows and arrows had been cached in the stronghold at daybreak; no arms were carried, not even lances.

117

Before mid-forenoon the little plaza of Santa Rita was a moving crowd; vinto tinto and dulce was brought in tubs and mescal in earthen jugs, and oxen were skewered on great poles and turned over the fire with the strength of men and boys. The shops were also crowded.

Juan Jose, in eagle feathers and a green bar of high privilege across his left cheek, took his seat at the flowing center of his feast. Santa Rita's alcalde waddled out to mollify with him. Red Sleeve, with a small globe of vermillion on his right arm (the red shirt having long since ravelled into dust) was greeted by the Padre. Presently the leader of the white party rocked laughing into the plaza, several of his men about him. Swaying and roaring with laughter, the leader appeared as high host of the day, above the Alcalde, even above the Medicine Padre. He jostled the senoritas who screamed with pleasure. He reached for young squaws, who were never there when his hands closed to take them, but he caught up one papoose, big enough to work his own legs but not fast enough to get away, and tossed him aloft, setting him back on the earth, stunned with fright and his mother also. His eyes glared whitely; his face seemed made of two parts that did not belong together. The knees of Red Sleeve weakened as he came near.

"Senor John-sohn!" cried the Alcalde. "Senor John-sohn!"

But Red Sleeve named him "Senor Two Face," and life departed from his knees as he watched. Plenty mescal did not soothe this strange untamable disquiet.

The sky held no cloud.

The squaws gazed upon the Mexican women, especially watching the younger Mexican women in their white dresses and black mantillas. Then the squaws looked down at themselves with misgiving. They did not appear the same to themselves, as when they started out in the morning. One young squaw, in the midst of Mimbreno women, swaying her hips as the senoritas did, looked back over her legs behind. This was not Firefly, but to do this was not unlike Firefly, with no papoose to hold her hand or bend her back, and not a day older or fatter than the evening he first skited gravel at her feet. And Placid sat with her own growing ones about her, and her back was broad with bearing and other labor, but he liked not her breed and would never have seen her, save through the eyes of another, now dead.

Also he saw the braves and older men of his people drinking mescal, eating chunks of beef hot from the fire, taking the smaller things of food that were passed them; but mainly he watched Juan Jose sitting broad like a carcass opened beneath, and taking his liquor like one who had looked toward this hour through many days of horse-killing raid. But Juan Jose had not come in from far travels; he had kindled no fires within him to meet the fires of mescal. The Alcalde came to sit with him for a moment; "Senor John-sohn" in his turn, and other trappers in theirs, all bringing honor of this great day to Juan Jose, whose day would be over at noon, since all his strength was the strength of sitting men only.

And Red Sleeve thought of the words that were still to be spoken; also he remembered the day he had brought furs to Santa Rita and received his money for them and much mescal afterward. Less and less did he belong to this feast, nor did he find it good to be apart like this, with all others forgetting. Much thinking alone by the fire had made him restive and solitary, so that he was not of his people on their great day.

He watched the face of the Medicine Padre under his black hat, and that face was whiter than ever and different from the hour of their arrival in the morning; yes, it was clear from the face of the Padre that this day was not unfolding according to the purpose laid down.

Red Sleeve moved to and fro, feeling the tramped earth with his feet and holding it firm beneath him, his knees not balancing easily, his eyes everywhere but showing nothing of what they saw. This was not like the day he drank with the Mexicans, for then he had only his own purse to save; but this day he had the will of all his people to hold to, since none other appeared called upon to remember.

One by one the braves were rolling over where they sat, the squaws slavering with drunkenness, and Juan Jose lay asleep with his women about him cleaning the ooze that pumped up on his face and neck as he breathed.

The sky burned in its unhampered light. With a loin of hot meat in his hands, Red Sleeve moved to and fro— pushing past those who offered wine and mescal and further food. At a distance, near a great mound of soccoro piled in bags and covered with green branches, he saw "Senor Two Face" and the Alcalde talking. Their eyes moved to him and moved quickly away. His arms hung empty and useless beside him with no pesh-e-gar in the hollow of one or the other, and his shoulder felt the heat of the sun where no quiver of arrows rested. He ate the hot tender meat, but his stomach did not rise avidly to receive it. He tossed the loin to the dogs, drank a gourd of purple wine but it did not touch the disquiet in him.

The sun was well past noon. They were bringing bags of grain from the mounds under the green boughs, to the center of the plaza near where Juan Jose lay in the midst of the women. They were opening the bags and calling to the Mimbrenos to come and take what they could—presents of grain from Santa Rita to all Indian guests. The braves did not move, but squaws were taking off their skirts to make sacks for the corn.

Red Sleeve stood apart in disapprobation. He liked not to see his people moiling together like starving dogs. The Medicine Padre also walked alone, raising his hands to the sun; and over by the great pile of soccoro, "Senor Two Face" was lighting a cigarito with a great laugh. All this, Red Sleeve saw in the full light of unshadowed sky, his eyes being secretly open, as one who walks ways that are retained in memory afterward.

Such was the culminating instant of the feast of Santa Rita, when a crashing peal of thunder burst from the earth, and invisible death of lightning struck the plaza.

Many of his people were leveled with the stroke, but they had not merely fallen. They were hacked and broken, chopped and spotted and writhing together over the spilled corn. It came again with no cloud of warning—a second thundering belch from the earth and another great swathe of his people cut to the plaza turf. That which had been Juan Jose and five women, was but the centerpiece of a wide carpet of butchered Mimbrenos.

His own household was like Juan Jose's, and many others, though at the edges of the great reaping strokes, many Mimbrenos were rising and running away.

Then he saw that the pile of soccoro was breaking down—that Mexican soldiers and white men were pouring forth to finish the destruction which the angry gods began.

Before him on the ground was a child rising like a calf, hind feet first. He caught it up and stampeded with the others toward the small trees where the Indian ponies were tethered. Everywhere the firing of the Mexicans and whites followed him; with others of his people it was the same, each Apache a darting rabbit, hounds closing in wherever he turned.

He passed the Medicine Padre on his knees calling upon the Virgin, his hands striking the earth before him, the face of one whose bare back is pressed upon the torture cactus. He heard the shots and screams of the continued butchering behind. Now, as he approached the picket line where the ponies were tethered, the Mexicans opened fire from there. He turned back, running another way, and to the side he saw "Senor Two Face" following him with a rifle point, the two parts of his face far apart in the powder smoke.

XXIX

Though he seemed to be running in the thick of night, there was daylight far above among the Mimbreno tee-pees. The old ones there who had not gone to the feast were peering down as he came. Aña was there, standing motionless, looking from his face to the thing in his arms. Standing before her thus, he began to come to himself—panting like a horseless stripling, a papoose in his arms like a squaw. He halted, plumped the papoose to the ground, and looked back.

It was not yet night. Hours still were left of this same unclouded day—this the day of the end and the beginning. He vanished into the larger teepee and stood silently in the dusk for several moments, recollecting himself. He knew the shame of the Apache who has been stampeded—off his feet, off his head. But Aña alone had seen him running and halting, like one full grown in body, but partly grown in brain, a papoose in his arms; she alone had seen the night in his eyes while it was yet day. He picked up his rifle and powder pouch, and crowded out through the flap again, taking his stand by the ashes of his own fire, as the gasping survivors reached sanctuary.

They gathered about him, but not too near. He began counting them as they came. His eyes filled with them—the braves who had not rushed in to gather the corn. They saw him standing with his rifle and went to the cache of their bows and arrows. Now the wounded were coming up and the squaws and children who had not

been able to crowd so close to the opened bags of corn—
those who had outrun the fire of the Mexican soldiers.
He counted them in tens.

Including the Warm Springs squaws and children,
nearly eight hundred Mimbrenos had crowded into Santa
Rita. Of these, nearly two hundred had remained at the
feast; of that number, three-fourths were squaws and
children.

After many moments of counting, he stood and looked
again over the faces of the waiting warriors; and still it
was a company struck dumb. He could understand that.
It had been so in himself. Night had also fallen upon
him with full day abroad. To him, as to all his people,
that which is unforeseen is the deadliest enemy, the surest,
the only disruption. Most of those before him when
night had fallen, had been plucked suddenly from the
stupor of drunkenness.

Yet now the time had come; he alone was prepared.
Not one of the faces before him had seen his undoing;
they had seen only their own, and that of their women
and children when death fell in the plaza. He glanced
at the sun; his eye swept down over the copper camp
below, and beyond into Sonora on the right hand, beyond
into Chihuahua on the left hand. He turned and gazed
upon the mountains of the Chihuicahuis. His feet pressed
the earth of his own place. He raised his hand and the
globe of red upon the flat of his forearm caught the eyes
of his people. Murmuring subsided; groans were hushed.

". . . Copper Mine Mimbreno no more watch Nakai-yi
miner pick cobre from the mountain. No more watch
senorita put her feet down different from Mimbreno
girl. No more drink mescal in shops or make trade for

white iron. Feast day come, feast day go—all Mimbreno warrior on warpath now."

So brief the peroration, as Mangus Colorado in the full prime of his manhood, nearer forty than thirty, assumed command of his people. Quickly he explained there was no time for war dance; Ne-pot-on-je, Medicine chief of the Mimbrenos, had not returned from the plaza. His eye turned to the low head of Wano-boono, and others of the Medicine Lodge for sanction to his word that war was now entered upon without preliminary.

"The spirits of our people already moving in the night-wind attest to this," said Wano-boono; thus the strength of the Medicine Lodge became his.

"Night come soon; bring no fires to this place," he resumed. "Mimbreno no longer stay in stronghold here. Mexican soldier maybe come and burn teepees. Wounded Mimbreno go to Dark Canyons, where water make no sound. If Mexican soldiers come there, Mimbreno boy and girl run away; other Mimbreno kill wounded who cannot run and hide."

Followed his assignments to action—names not chosen at random, but of those he had long watched and whose qualities he had weighed—all young men upon whom he had fixed for honors and for molding into his plans.

"Delgadito!"

A nephew of Juan Jose stepped forward. Mangus Colorado pointed southwest to Sonora.

"Three, four, five sun's jornada, Cuchillo Negro with Warm Springs braves coming this way. Delgadito swift ride, no stop. Carry word of Mangus Colorado to Cuchillo Negro—word of feast of Santa Rita—word of end of feast. Big conducta coming this way. Cuchillo

Negro surprise and kill. Take no prisoners, leave no one to bring word to Janos, no one to come and tell Santa Rita. Take all guns, powder, ball, knives, horses, mules, burn *ilge-nad-in* (trash). Cache treasure in Mimbreno hiding places and come this way, all eyes upon the road!"

He called Coletto Amarillo (Yellow Tail) and two other young men, sending them north into the Pinos Altos to join up with the scouts watching the second party of fifteen "Go-dammies" coming toward the Copper Mines. His order was that word be brought back to him at once of the place of their camp tonight. He then turned to the southeast where shone the mountains of Chihuahua now warmly bright in a haze of western light. The Apache name he now spoke was of that young warrior known as Victorio afterward.

"Braves to number of five tens catch horses now—make ride to White Eagle Pass—wait for conducta coming this way—"

He reiterated the orders given to Delgadito that concerned extermination, caching of treasure, vigilance, traveling light, and the postponement of all feasting, drinking, until a united Mimbreno people looked down upon the plaza of Santa Rita and knew that the terrible score was settled. Another party of fifty, under No-po-so was to wait only for full darkness, before closing in on the road to Janos, destroying any living thing that moved upon it north or south.

From all outgoing parties he demanded runners to be sent back frequently. For years his thoughts had secretly moved as one already in command. His various orders covered smallest details. His people moved before him like grass in the fanning of wind, like water to the slope of the land—moved in different directions to carry out his thoughts. Exactly as he was prepared to rule, these minds were ready to receive the impregnation of his will.

Still he saw looped in every eye and checked on every lip, the question: "What was the nature of that which fell upon us in the plaza of the feast?"

The answer to that question he did not know himself. What the gods had done in the beginning was one thing, but of a certainty the Nakai-yes and "Los Go-dammies," had worked with the gods to carry on the destruction. He knew no more than this. A warrior standing at the outer edge of the Mimbrenos gave a sudden signal for silence. Mangus Colorado moved toward him, the crowd parting to let him pass. He looked down, following the quick gesture of the other.

A solitary figure coming up the trail from Santa Rita— black clothed and hatted—carrying neither cross nor cloth of white.

A low murmur of protest started behind him. He turned and it fell to silence, even the movements of lip erased. He went back to the ashes of his fire to wait, and even yet the sun still lingered above the mountains of the Chihuicahuis.

"Don-Ha! Don-Ha!" cried a voice from the shadowy trail below.

XXX

THE OLD MAN bowed with climbing raised himself on
the ridge. His eyes looked sightless for an instant as the
last rays of sun filled them. The Mimbrenos drew back,
a sound of hissing on their lips—thumbs and little fingers
of their hands pointing at his waist and limbs, their
cheeks drawn back and tongues loosely visible. He was
loathsome disease to their eyes. That his body held together was an affront to their deepest instincts.

At the end of the lane of Mimbrenos, Padre's eyes fixed
upon him whom he sought. His stiffened limbs moved
woodenly forward. He knelt at the very moccasins of
the great figure standing.

"My gods have mocked me. My people have used me
as a tool for their destruction. Do with me what you
will, Don-Ha!"

Mangus Colorado let the Padre stay where he was.

". . . There was left only for me to come and lay my
heart at the feet of the friend I have so sorely wronged."

Mangus Colorado sat down before the stones of his fire-
place. The wind eddied among the cold ashes. He
looked into the darkened flap of the larger teepee where
Firefly and Placid and the small children would not return. Sufficient orders had been given to the Mimbrenos
for the present; he waved them away. Time now to learn
what manner of thing had taken place in the plaza of the
feast. The Padre spoke again.

". . . A second time that which was to be the fruit of

128

my birth is withered and full of bitterness. I have wrought in my own way and not God's way—"

It had always been so. Always many words to listen to, before that which signified was brought to speech. The Padre would speak of the virgin, doubtless. The night wind stirred the low brush. The day had darkened; there was no fire between them. The old ache of listening was sudden detestation to Mangus Colorado now, but he waited for the Padre to be silent. At length his arm raised and his finger pointed to the sky slightly to the west of meridian.

"The day before this day, when the sun was there, Medicine Padre came to his friend with words of friendship."

"Si, si, Don-Ha—"

"Medicine Padre invited his friend and all Mimbreno people to a feast."

"Si, si, Don-Ha, I was duped! The people of Sonora prevailed wickedly upon my people to use me to bring you to the fiesta. I did not know then that the white men had promulgated a plan with the soldiers and miners to destroy my friend and his people. It was brought to me that this was to be a feast of reconciliation, a truce that would never be broken, and that I should carry the invitation."

Mangus Colorado bowed his head to hide the snapping of his eyes.

"That which I desired to believe, I believed so ardently, that the truth evaded my eyes."

"Medicine Padre know his gods better than he know his own people."

"God forgive me—what you say is true, Don-Ha."

"The name of this Indian has not been Don-Ha for long time."

"Si—Mangus Colorado, but the name of your boyhood returns to my lips. May the Mother of Christ—"

"Medicine Padre say 'Los Go-dammies' talk this thing with Mexican soldier and Mexican miner?"

"It was the thought of the white men first. It was 'Senor John-sohn' who told the miners that he knew a way to rid Santa Rita of Apache trouble for all time. Also he said he had come without furs, hearing of the new Sonora law—"

Mangus Colorado looked down upon Santa Rita del Cobre. "White men no longer sell animal furs—sell Indian hair—" he said.

"I ran among them crying against it! They laughed, saying 'Why should we take furs of animals when Apache scalps are worth a hundred and fifty pesos, squaw scalps a hundred pesos, and the scalps of Apache children, fifty pesos?' Such was the plan of 'Senor John-sohn'—may God have mercy on his soul—scalps in great number for the price of a few bags of corn; meanwhile to give such a lesson to the Apaches that they would never again come near the mines of Santa Rita."

Mangus Colorado sombrely said: "White man very wise. White man well say Mimbreno never go to Santa Rita plaza any more. Big thunder come—no cloud in the sky. Big lightning cut down Mimbreno Indian. Medicine Padre now tell Indian friend what medicine white hunters used to bring so much quick death to Santa Rita plaza."

"A pair of two-wheeled howitzers—not medicine, Mangus Colorado—brought from the barracks at Janos, loaded with powder and then to the muzzle with slugs, nails and bullets! These were concealed in the branches and bags of corn. It was 'Senor John-sohn' who thought of this terrible thing and wrought with his friends and the soldiers and miners to finish the work. It was 'Senor John-sohn' who set off the fuses."

The thick iron reeds on wagons.

The Mimbreno considered at length. What he had required to know was now learned, but there was left a great darkness and bitterness from the telling. Wagons that spat out lightning like the very gods in anger; wagons that carried great tubes like a hundred pesh-e-gar in one. Against his own strength, against the power to carry out his thoughts, against the bright grain at the core of his mind—the future as never before suddenly showed black. As his knees had weakened at the sight of the white men in the plaza, his spirit quailed before the unthinkable resources of the new enemy. Yet quietly he said: "Mimbreno Indian now go away on long journey where Nakai-yi no come—where 'Los Go-dammies' no can find. Is all now said between Medicine Padre and his friend?"

"All but one thing, Mangus Colorado! Nothing for myself. Life is nothing to me—indeed, the end is come. When the light goes out of the house, though movement is heard, the house is empty. Yet a word of your forgiveness, Mangus Colorado, if only for the good of *your* soul—only that, before you let your people do with me what they will."

The Mimbreno's anger mounted. Of all the Padre's foolishness, this was the head and face. To be forgiven— the Mimbrenos would roll about in the earth laughing at that. To be forgiven not for Padre's peace, but for the good of the Mimbreno! Mangus Colorado contained himself in silence, yet he wanted the Medicine Padre out of the sight of his eyes. Allegiance to this man had rendered him powerless in the plaza, had rendered nameless all the clamor of warnings in his brain before the slaughter.

Suddenly his body shook; a shudder vibrated from the base of his spine; his voice rumbled abruptly: "Night has come. No fires burn in Indian Camp. No light shine in Indian teepee. Mimbreno squaw in Nakai-yi plaza stuck in blood. Papoose lay close—no milk. Papoose head bare to dark and cold. Mimbreno brave lay in same place—no hair. Head of brave, head of squaw, head of papoose bare to wind and dark. Spirit run out quick when Indian hair is taken. Spirit come quick to Mimbreno camp—papoose, squaw and brave run back here—no fire to warm—shiver in wind. Mimbreno alive run to far mountains—no look back— shiver and shake—no get free from Mimbreno dead running after in wind.

". . . Medicine Padre come up Indian trail alone. Mimbreno people want to kill Medicine Padre. Mangus Colorado say no. Medicine Padre no die here. Friend no kill friend. Indian no slay friend who come to tell his fault. Medicine Padre ask forgive. Mimbreno dead no forgive. Mimbreno alive no forgive. . . . Medicine Padre go now. Say Indian go to far mountains. No come again to Mexican plaza for a feast."

He arose and turned his back.

XXXI

Mangus Colorado sat in the windy dark and followed in his thoughts the outrushing lines of his warriors—one to Chihuahua, one to find private perches in the hills overlooking the road to Janos, one connecting up with the fifteen whites back in high country. Other warriors were now sent below to reconnoitre Santa Rita and report the slightest move of departure on the part of the Mexicans or whites under "Senor Two Face."

Also he considered Cuchillo Negro afar in Sonora and the women and children and wounded on the way to Dark Canyons. Aña was with them and with her was the small one of Placid's bringing plucked from the plaza. Twice that small one had passed through the teeth of the comb from the fire wagons, a boy-papoose, if memory served correctly. There was now no other, Firefly having brought forth trouble only and the scalding of those near. Still no other had known her.

On better thought he recalled that there was a thin squalling kitten in Aña's arms; another coming possibly. The Mimbrenos were running low on squaws, low on ninyas: the feast had taken all too many of the latter as they preened in the plaza. Time to consider that dearth when Apache law was satisfied. Still, ninyas would be much wanted when the time came.

His mind reviewed the firing of the Mexicans and others upon his Mimbrenos who escaped death from the fire wagons. As a whole the Apache could have done better than that, but there was one memorable point to be considered. Darting toward the small trees where the Indian ponies were tethered, he had met the fire of the whites from the picket line. "Senor Two Face" had thought of posting men there doubtless; certainly no Mexican.

Finally he fell to pondering upon himself, here in the dark, as the center-point of all Mimbrenos. Wherever he was, there was the center-point, the thought in the brain of every warrior now turning back to him. What he thought of alone, they thought and talked of afterward together. He held all the lines; he sat in the brain of every warrior. It had long been coming; there had been no question when the time arrived.

Yes, there had been question, when he permitted the Medicine Padre to enter and depart alive, when all Mimbrenos hungered and thirsted to hear the Padre's voice a last time head down over a slow fire. Then there had been question.

Half-Foot, one of those returned from the plaza doubtless questioned that, and other medicine men. Cuchillo Negro would question that when he came in, even as he had questioned the weaknesses of Juan Jose, and his father before him. Moreover, Cuchillo Negro would question the orders sent from "Mangus Colorado," but the report of the feast in the plaza and the killing of many Warm Springs squaws and children would set him to work carrying out those orders instantly.

After that Cuchillo Negro and this center-point of all Mimbrenos would come together and each would know who the other was, and where he belonged, and the people would know also.

At midnight his first scout returned with word of the

camping place of the whites. Leaving another of his favorites, called Ponce, in command of the basic position, he followed the runner back into the mountains.

Presently he began to know a strange lightness of limb as he followed the brave before him. From a boy he had heard men speak of this—the new life that takes the Indian when the warpath is entered; even at the war dance of preparation, often. One might fatten in camp for many moons, yet be suddenly inspirited.

A spanking of nettles, the warpath.

Surely an Apache was one thing when his teepees were raised for sitting; on the warpath quite another.

And this war-taking of all Mimbrenos had come without war dance or conjuring of medicine or asking of moon or star. In the plaza of feasting, in the stupor of drunkenness to many; to all who had not known death, it had come. And here moving in the dark was the center-point of all war to be made; wherever he moved was that center-point.

The sweat of suppleness was upon him. Though it was full dark in the canyons, his feet found the silent places among twig and leaf and stone. The scout was leading noiselessly. Down slopes of loose shale, not the least slide was started. Pesh-e-gar clinked against no branch or rock wall. In the density of night before the day-gray, they saw their way. An owl hooted. It was not necessary.

Already Mangus Colorado smelled the faint sweetness of wood-smoke from the camp at the foot of the canyon. No Apache would make a camp there, where voices had to be raised above the chatter of water. He saw a flutter of sparks, as a gust of wind uncovered the ashes. That was like white men, building such a great fire the night before that it would still spark when dawn was at hand. Their beasts had not been turned loose to graze.

He peered down long. One of the trappers was awake, sitting hunched, head covered; others lay as if trussed under their blankets. He had now come into the cordon of his own warriors. He felt the rocky earth giving off its dawn-chill. The cold hung in a heavier layer down where the white men lay. They camped at the water's very edge, as if afraid it would all run away if they left. They camped where the light came last and the warmth came last.

As the night thinned, he ranged his warriors on shelving balconies, and sent one party up and another down the canyon to cut off retreat. Not a word was spoken; they watched the slightest move of his hand. His own rifle would be the signal. One of the mules below raised its head and began sawing forth its song. The sentry growled his favorite words—and heaved a rock at the mule. The others stirred. One sat up and shivered. "Jesus!" he said.

Mangus Colorado would have waited several minutes later for clearer light, but it was now time, while they were dull-witted from sleep and before they located their rifles. He took careful aim at the sentry and fired.

Arrows sped down into the blankets; at the instant of release the war whoop sounded. Those below were on their feet now, darting about, piling over each other. Some of them reached for their hats and pulled them on before taking up their rifles. The sentry was on his hands and knees waving his head toward water like a gopher bitten by a rattlesnake. Others were running down to the mouth of the canyon; others up toward the bend; warriors waiting at either end. The mules had broken loose, threshing about in the water, over the blankets and cooking pots.

Several of the trappers were on their knees or huddled against the canyon walls, looking up for something to fire at. One was crying out and crossing himself like the Medicine Padre. He was one chosen for a bullet, clean and quick—the third of Mangus Colorado's own. Another held up his arms empty-handed; a black beard, very narrow at the eyes. The arrows rained upon him. He drew a short gun from his belt and opened his mouth to it, as if drinking from a bottle.

When all was still the Apaches went down to them. Mangus Colorado pointed out the several works of his rifle. He chose the short gun of the black-bearded one for his own belt. The arrows were re-gathered and dried before the sinews loosened from the points. There was little time to play among the bodies. All were accounted for; also rifles and extra rifles. There was much powder and ball, but little provisions. The mules were caught and loaded.

XXXII

Kites and buzzards circled in clouds over the copper camp and the village itself. The teepees overlooking Santa Rita were abandoned, nor were any erected elsewhere at this time. The old ridge hangout was now a stench to Mimbreno nostrils, as if the fumes of the plaza rose to it.

The new base became a shifting one in the fresh rocky country to the north; yet scouts under strictest cover kept watch at the old resort, on the lookout for any courier coming in from his three detachments to the south. Mangus Colorado's orders were that no movements were to be made except in full stalking stealth. His runners followed the arroyos; no ponies were used; his spies commanded the landscape from every peak. He lit no smoke or signal fires, wishing to carry out exactly the word planted with Padre Font that the Mimbrenos had fled to far places, goaded by the haunting of their dead.

Cuchillo Negro with his hundred or more Warm Springs Apaches was relied upon to do his part without supervision. Sonora would have something fresh to talk about each day with the wrath of Black Knife now in full working order. As for the parties watching the Janos road under No-po-so, and the one farther afield toward Chihuahua under Victorio, Mangus Colorado's confidence was not established to the same degree. He kept runners going to them with further inspiriting commands, and demands for information on all that took place. Meanwhile he was tirelessly afoot. Years of na-tse-kes, the turning over and over again of his thoughts, had now given way to carrying out his thoughts one by one.

Everywhere he was treated with great respect; approached and addressed with ceremony. This had been growing upon all his people through the hours. His leadership was instantly accepted, but adjustments to it were slightly slower in the minds of his people. This was the third great step of his rise; the first from the corn-watcher to the bringer-in of the Pattie treasure single-handed; the second, from hesitation before the knife duel with Pindah, to him who had visibly risen to invincibility and slain the son of Soldado Fiero without a scratch to his own body; the third, his assumption as war-chief as darkness fell after the feast in the plaza. He was actually seen as a different man. Further steps were matters of prophecy only and distant looming.

There was additional reason for ceremonial and profound formality. This had to do with the abrupt entering of the warpath by the whole Mimbreno nation. All that had to do with war was now spoken of in a different tone, called by a different name frequently. The word "chief" was prefixed to that of the leader, and "brave" to the warrior. A pony became a charger in effect; lances, arrows, bows were in a measure sanctified. Matters of march and camp, dress and decorum took on a religious significance. All that would hamper the utmost mobility was discarded; all the rest consecrated to one great end.

Mangus Colorado went into Dark Canyons to look after his people there. The wounded were many. Some few had lived only to reach that retreat; rock piles now marked their bodies. Others were stretched out in the long fight to live, not having yet met the crisis. Old Calico Turkey and Half-Foot and other medicine people ministered to these.

Aña was there, washing at the stream bank, when he came. Her body unbent from the water, her eyes came up to her lord, the fear never fully gone from them. She stood waiting his word, her body ripened with young. On the gravel at her feet was one of hers, the bird-faced tinito that he had not observed closely until now. Yes, a ninya-bud; he had been quite sure of that. Still ninyas would be much in demand among the Mimbrenos from now on.

"Muchachito?" he questioned, thinking of the one he had plucked from the Plaza.

She pointed down the stream a little way where Placid's boy-papoose sat in shallow water, slapping it about him as if it were his own. Mangus Colorado looked at that young one, then back at Aña. He looked her over from head to foot until her eyes turned down to the water. Gruffly he asked if all was right with her.

"Si, Senor. Very good."

He had not observed her so closely like this for many days. Her eyes opened more widely than any of the squaws; she could not keep them hidden away about their own affairs as did his own people. She saw no more, nor so much as Indian women, yet what she saw was no secret to another. Her garments were clean, even in the turmoil of this hasty refuge.

He spoke softly for no one else to hear, "Chief of all Mimbrenos—me—huh!"

She signified that she had heard so from many lips. She had also heard him give his commands as darkness fell on feast day. He turned away. This was no time to be looking on a woman.

"Cafe, Senor?" she questioned.

"Huh—no cafe here."

"Si, senor." She ran to her uncovered packs and brought forth a little sack, not much bigger than hodden-tin bag.

"Cafe bueno," he said. "This Indian go soon."

She was already stirring the fire. The coffee was properly cooled when he returned for a survey of camp and a word with Calico Turkey and Half-Foot. He drank it to the last drop and departed.

XXXIII

A FTER sundown that night, Mangus Colorado left Ponce in command at the base, and went alone down trail toward the lights of Santa Rita. Nearing the village, he circuited to the east and came up to it again from the desert side, following an arroyo. Closer and closer he crept until not only the lights but the lamps were seen through the doorways. He heard the strum of a guitar and a man and a woman singing together. They sang of the dove and the lark.

Voices reached him from the mescal shops. "Los Godammies" were there, and in and out of the streets, hailing the miners and calling to the senoritas. The little plaza was now crowded with living again; music sounded from shadowed, dobe walls. There were lights in the mission, figures hurrying in to pray. Presently from there came singing—of Maria, the Virgin, of course. They knew no other than that, and of the blood of her son, "Sangre de Christo."

Lights burned in the house from which Aña had been taken. Farther on began the slope to the three-walled presidio; soldiers sitting at the gate, a sentry walking up and down; none but soldiers could go that way. One of them began singing:

"Que el Yaqui sabe morir."

More than once he had heard that before.

Farther back a great laugh sounded in the plaza. That was the white man's way of singing. He licked his dry dusty lips, creeping nearer. Breast down, he heard the

142

tread of feet on the earth, the stamping of horses and mules in the corrals, and the quick beat of running pads— a coyote pack farther out in the desert. Then the smells of the village passed out of his nostrils—smells of carne, of mescal, ron blanco, tobaho, stables, wood fire and out-houses—all swallowed up in one heavy hanging taint.

Now the sand was pitted and overturned. He saw the long trenches loosely filled in. This was where they had taken the bodies from the plaza. This was where the kites and buzzards had concentrated in their hanging aloft through the long day.

No party had left Santa Rita. No pack-train was in the plaza preparing for journey tomorrow. He had estimated the number of the people as over three hundred, including the women and children. Miners and soldiers and whites numbered half this amount. He would account for them later one by one. Now far back at the barracks several soldiers had taken up the song the one began:

"La raza de bronce que sabe morir—" (The bronze race that knows how to die.)

XXXIV

Mangus Colorado was gone less than three hours, but in the meantime a runner had come in from No-po-so in command of the watchers of the Janos road, and was keeping himself awake to make report. Ponce also stated that the Medicine Padre had come up the trail alone, and upon reaching the ridge had called the name "Mangus Colorado" not loudly but in the tone of mighty grief. He had then made signs in the sky, doubled himself on the ground and departed as he came. The Mimbrenos had not made answer.

The runner from the Janos party reported that a small pack-train on the way into the Copper Mines had been waylaid and destroyed early this morning in the mountains forty miles this side of Janos. The mules were used to carry the packs into an Apache cache in the mountains. Much food, guns and ammunition, and mescal in great earthen casks wrapped in reed, were included in the treasure taken; also six senoritas en route for Santa Rita. Mangus Colorado inquired what time of day the attack on the pack-train had taken place.

"At the break of this day."

He now ascertained the number of casks of mescal, and inquired if any of these had been broached before the mountain cache was reached. The runner was not sure, having left shortly after the attack was finished. Mangus Colorado inquired if all the prisoners were put to death at once. The answer was that the six senoritas were not dead when he left; that there was talk of keeping them alive until night.

The chief fell to pondering. Presently he noted the runner still standing before him. This man had done sixty miles in the last eleven hours, his horse having lasted little more than half the distance. He was now permitted to sleep.

Ponce was called. The two sat in silence and darkness. This young man was not unreservedly to the liking of the leader, flighty and unstabilized, but of the authority of warrior blood. Mangus Colorado presently spoke of certain matters he had observed in Santa Rita, and that Usen had his eyes on the Mimbrenos at this time as never before. The fact that there had been no formal consecration to war in the way of dance did not make less solemn the present crisis; this crisis, in fact, was prepared for through many years, the future of all Mimbrenos depending upon the complete dedication of every living tribesman.

Ponce listened in silence. Such words as these would not now be necessary, said Mangus Colorado, save for an affair not to his liking in the party of No-po-so in the Janos direction. If one returned from there within the next two or three days, he was to be sent to Dark Canyons with the wounded and the women. At this time, he Mangus Colorado, must rise and go to that hiding place. Affairs here accordingly depended upon Ponce's vigilance, acumen and sleepless concentration.

The young warrior gravely accepted the responsibility. Mangus Colorado then said that the Medicine Padre was ready for death; that his greatest punishment was to remain alive; that it was well he had been permitted to call without answer and depart without harm. The Medicine Padre alone should be unmolested in case of departure from Santa Rita in any direction; but those with him should be taken, except in the cases of the parents and brothers of Aña; these if possible should remain unharmed, no other exceptions among the Nakai-yes. In all cases of those attempting to leave Santa Rita, the attack upon them should be postponed until they were at a considerable distance from the village; all vigilance should be used to prevent the escape of any members of any party back to Santa Rita.

Mangus Colorado now came to a point of great importance. He desired to be present and direct affairs in case of departure of "Senor Two Face" and the whites. He did not believe they would leave Santa Rita immediately, but if they did leave while he was away, they should be followed closely and runners sent back to this place, the attack upon them delayed if possible until his return. If it were not feasible to delay attack to this length, prisoners should be taken in this case and no other.

Ponce declared himself conversant with these details. Taking Coletto Amarillo with two of the best ponies, Mangus Colorado then headed south at once. Nine hours later, two hours after daybreak, he was signaled by a pair of No-po-so's scouts, five miles north of the main Apache position above the Janos road. He was now riding Coletto Amarillo's horse, his own having given out hours before under his great weight and the unremitting speed of the journey. His second mount was also tottering and done-for. Coletto Amarillo was miles behind on foot.

The two scouts were dull-witted from mescal. Mangus Colorado said nothing, left his pony for them to finish and stalked into the camp of No-po-so alone on foot. He was enabled to come upon it without challenge. He was within easy rifle shot of the young leader himself before his coming was apprehended.

Those few of the men who had awakened by this time, might as well have been asleep, their heads steaming with mescal fumes. Fires had been built the night before. One of No-po-so's braves was dead and two badly wounded—not from battle capturing the Mexican pack-train but from fighting each other in the night. The bodies of the senoritas were flung aside uncovered; one of these was still warm. The disgrace was complete, except for the one detail that No-po-so himself was not drunk. He hung his hard compact head, his mouth was compressed, making no defense in word or gesture.

XXXV

THE SUN was high. Mangus Colorado rode alone to
the east and south. In his night traveling he had foreseen that this was to be a day of great heat, and before
him to cross was a valley of fire, nearly a hundred miles
without water or shade. He had not tarried at the camp
of No-po-so, only to await the coming of Coletto
Amarillo, and leave a thorn of lasting rectitude against
the spine of spine of No-po-so, and those not too drunk
to listen to a few well-studied words.

Only to see that no mescal remained unpoured on the
ground, and to perfect a cache for remaining matters of
the train for future examination and use of the tribe.

The earth heated as if the desert were one vast maguay
bake. The birds grew silent and all living things were
tranced in the burning; only the lizards that are born of
wrath were not crisped.

Among the new horses in No-po-so's hiding place was a
mature dun-colored mare ridden by the Mexican boss-
packer at the time of attack yesterday morning. This
Mangus Colorado had perceived at the time No-po-so first
hung his head; and this he had taken to himself at that
moment in his thoughts. She was a full hand's-breadth
taller than the run of Apache ponies and full-bodied to
match; there was a gleam in her eye that he had seen
in Firefly's and wanted without reason. No-po-so said
the nan-tan of the pack-train had died gazing upon this
mare, his lips moving with a name that No-po-so had not
remembered.

Mostly to Apaches who are horse raiders, not horse breeders, a pony is just a pony, as one coin is like another. A faulty eye, a shortened tendon or a bone-deep gall nicks the coin out of circulation, in which case it goes to the butcher; otherwise all ponies look alike, but this mare awakened Mangus Colorado.

She was restless to go before the saddle settled; he was glad to have her alone, having set out on the Jornado del Muerto, cutting across open desert from the Janos road to that used by the conductas between Santa Rita and Chihuahua. The mare found her stamina, only to lose it again trying to get rid of this weight of two men in one. She tried everything she knew, charging a low-hung sahuara branch to rake him off. She fell into a long frictionless lope, stealing speed on a hard-packed stretch, then suddenly bolted, expecting to see him sail overhead. Instead, her ribs were suddenly clamped in forceps of a man-power unfelt heretofore.

Mangus Colorado mightily approved. "Ko-do," he called her, glancing back at her plump hips where began the coils of power that shoved the desert behind her. He knew what was going on in her head by the play of her ears. He had felt her unparalleled speed as she craftily let herself out to bolt. She was faded dull now, but would be full black in winter and shiny velvet in spring. She had an eye of pure divination for gopher holes and loose stones. Her round hooves rattled steadily as pebbles in a gourd. She had wanted greatly to go, having been retarded for days by a pack-train of exceeding slowness. He knew now by her ears she was doing some serious thinking—no more wasting of strength in foolishness. This was a day of life or death; tardily she began to know it. It had taken five ponies to buy Placid, and naturally more to obtain the daughter of Soldado Fiero, a chieftain, but no woman was worth a mare like this. Time and place for all things, however.

He kept her at a steady lope. Yes, someone before him had liked her well; the saddle itself was worth a common pony; the bridle another, with silver coins worked into the leather. The reins were supple and well-tended. The Mexican saddle blanket was a satisfaction in itself.

Of the seven days of great heat that make the core of summer, there is one of stillest, deadliest wrath. The Mimbrenos always watched for the coming of this one day, and mostly had met it in late years by crawling down into the deep canyons, hanging over dim pools. This day found them abroad on the warpath, in full smiting blast from above and below.

It was now noon. He had done forty miles in three hours. For three hours more the burning would increase. The country was waterless to the distant mountains—the Sierra Madres, the Nakai-yes called them—a tinted glaze fifty miles away.

He thought of No-po-so going back to the Copper Mines on foot to hang his head among the women and the wounded; of No-po-so's men all seared and fevered from mescal and from fighting among themselves, the fighting of tontos (fools) only; of Coletto Amarillo perched like a young eagle over the Janos road and profiting by the mistakes of others. Orders would adequately be listened to hereafter. This was no Juan Jose giving orders and trusting to hearsay as to their carrying out.

No one would leave Santa Rita in heat like this. Last

night there had been no preparations for journey visible there. He thought of the Medicine Padre climbing the trail to call "Mangus Colorado" with a half-hundred ears to listen and not a lip to answer. His Virgin would hear the Medicine Padre only.

The sky was a burning glass that focalized upon the Chihuahua desert. A jack rabbit lay limp in the shade of a grease-wood, the pale roof of its mouth showing as it gasped in the broiling air. It slid out from underfoot with a half-dead fling. The thin strip of buckskin that had been tight about Mangus Colorado's temples in the morning, softened and slid out of place. This was all he wore to the waist; then breech-clout, leggings and snub-nosed moccasins of the warpath. Back of his deep shaded eyes, back of the eyeballs, was a fiery burning. It was there that the incessant activity told. The terrible wear of the day was felt, back against the brain.

The last of the plaza feast was sweated out by this time. His body hugged every drop of moisture that was left. He carried water—a length of horse intestine tied with buckskin at either end, but it would be greasy hot; he had not yet unbound it from the cantle. The thirst was passing out of his neck; that is but the first. The Apache prides himself on paying little attention to that. The second thirst is felt in the skin and deeper tissues; this calling of the blood for water can be borne. It is the third thirst, the thirst of the bones that becomes intolerable.

He was watching the mare; her pace not slackened, but she was tossing at the bit; her ears wilted, her hoof-beats unsteadied. He loosed her mouth and drew up his weight. Panic for breath, for water, for the end of running, panic of the desert, closed upon her. This was a crisis of her stretching; few beasts could have passed it; a lashing would have kept them on, but only to irretrievable ruin. His concern now was not to keep her on. It was an utterly novel concern that he had known only once before. The greatness of the dun mare was that she did not know how to slow down. Panic or not, she had no sense to quit. All her life with men she had been saved, pulled, held back. Now that she was given her will in one direction, she knew only to use it.

He watched the issue, forgetting the pitiless day. She steadied, found her wind again, the breath within the breath. She would be good for hours. She was drawing on rock-bottom now, the stamina of the great-hearted.

The withering gleam was at its height. He was trailing Victorio's band in a long dry water-course, parallel and a mile to the east of the Chihuahua road. He veered over to the main road, all "sign" there old and time-worn. Hazy skeletons of mesquite shadow marked the blistering sand. A stir of air. Now the mountains ahead were substance instead of ether-clots that dizzied the brain. The mare's head was outstretched. The bulge of her eye showed a glare; he heard the rasp of her breathing as the burden added on the up-trail.

That she did not come down of her own accord on the long upgrade—deepened her spell over him. The thing that he knew now was un-Apache. It was a concern for tomorrow. It linked him to the mystery of the corn-patch—novelty of unparalleled possession, an impulse at last to protect her—concern to save this creature from herself, to have her and not another for tomorrow. The inspired stimulus of the warpath—the venomous drive of speed and malice—was palliated to keep the mare alive. It was his hand that drew the rein.

That was not all. Her barrel rocked as she slackened to a trot; her blowing sounded louder as the rhythm was broken at last. He swung down and walked beside her hanging head. The bit hung loose in her shrunken gluey mouth. For one who had passed through the noon of today and lived, there was tangible coolness in the air. Shadows were longer; birds were coming to life in the brush. He took a deep draught of warm greasy water, then parted the gut for the mare. She shivered at the goading smell but sucked ravenously. Her heart was like a beating wing; yet no snuffle of leaky valve or blood-drenched lung marred the sound.

Victorio's band in Eagle Pass should "have" him by now. Still he cooled the mare, walking at her head. Entering the Pass, the mountains shut out the sun. He felt eyes upon him now, invisible as coyotes closing in. His mouth opened in a high thin yip-yiya-ha and his own Mimbrenos came to life about him eagerly. . . . A great conducta was coming from Chihuahua. Tonight its camp would be less than fifteen miles away on the far side of Cienaga Alta. Runners had been sent yesterday to the Copper Mines with this word.

One hundred and fifty miles since a little before last midnight; ninety miles in eight hours through this day, and the mare was still standing, weaving a little, but still on her very good feet. The like of her did not run the earth elsewhere. Ko-do, the firefly. No other should hear his name for her.

XXXVI

Victorio was hard and canny as a lodgepole pine. His camp was clean as a rain-washed leaf; like shadows about him were his swift and silent braves. Not a flick of wood-ash upon the ground. All were ready and glad for the eye of the new chief upon them. Where Victorio sat or stood, all others turned their faces, until Mangus Colorado came. Then Victorio turned his face from within himself, to his chieftain and other eyes followed. He spoke only the low inspired words of war. Night deepened with coolness. The thoughts of Mangus Colorado stood strongly forth that night; thoughts rapid and far-seeing; his body scoured gaunt from the journey did not obstruct his thought.

Coming to Victorio was meeting a friend after the desert.

Mangus Colorado moved apart and stood at the head of the dun mare. She was nosing for matters to her liking in the big forage pile before her. His fingers went over her nigh knee and she lifted the hoof to his hand. She nuzzled his clout for a present; doubtless she knew other things. He was getting to think well of one Mexican. He listened to her grinding and the active fluids at work upon the grist within. Time later to learn what more she could do. He would learn all her ways and teach her more, if paralysis did not catch her in the night.

Victorio brought cigaritos with papers of dried lily husks from the big cienaga near by. Victorio said that the pallet of Mangus Colorado was ready. He slept six hours, then made ready to accompany Victorio for a view of the conducta. The mare rose to her feet at his coming, as no foundered mare could do, though he had no thought to use her now.

Two hours later in the first light, his eyes filled with the great layout of the Nakai-yes—goods and animals and sleeping men. Including the soldiers in escort, the number of the pack-train outnumbered the Apaches. Breakfast fires were already being lighted below. It was like looking down upon Santa Rita itself—the massed fires at daybreak. Mantas and aparejos in long piles, groups of blanketed figures beginning to sit up—cafe, tortillas, huevos, steam of venison, pork and beef rising in the gray blue motionless air before sunrise.

This was not the place chosen for attack. The cienaga itself, seven miles farther back toward the Pass, exactly fitted the Apache idea for that. Mangus Colorado had passed by the cienaga in the dark this morning, and retraced now before the pack-train was in motion. The gorge widened into a mountain meadow, all but closed at either end. Cienaga Alta, high swamp, the Mexicans called it, but the Apaches had a more telling name, Womb of the Mountains.

He studied it in detail presently. The base of the gorge, where it widened like a big par-fleche, was edged with oak, alder, willow and buckthorn, admirably suited to ambuscade. The floor of the gorge was sludgy grass land—deeply mossed and lily covered, famed resting-ground for hoof-worn and travel-spent ponies. A few days here took the fever out of the joints and started the horn growing. Also the dried lily leaves were thin and tough and made better cigarito papers than even the husk of soccoro.

The day heightened, but not in the fury of yesterday. Sands of the journey of death yesterday; today water, wood and grass. Yet here, too, was high summer, the sun draining the trees of their life, even with their roots in water. The air was heavy-sweet with the essences of lily and fern and the bark of trees hard-pressed by the sun. Meanwhile the pack-train crawled nearer, Victorio and his men ranging above, muffle-winged like owls.

Now the train was filing into the cienaga, its ponderous length crowding in. Men and animals were glad for the soft giving carpet of moss and bordering shade. Victorio approached with word of his final readiness and silently departed, the face and bearing of a man who knew what he was about to do. The hollow of the gorge was crowded. It was mid-forenoon. Here a halt was to be made. At this moment the Nakai-yes relaxed the forward push and broke for shade. Mangus Colorado took aim at a Mexican officer in the lead. His shot was the signal.

At nightfall, he sat with Victorio among the rocks overlooking the cienaga. The peaks were darkening; night was thick below. Five Mimbrenos were dead, and twice as many lying with wounds. This matter was thoughtfully considered. Where many are killed, regardless of spoils, there is no victory. However, this number was not unseemly. Voices moaned up to the chief and his lieutenant from those Nakai-yes whom death had not yet silenced—women and children still hiding under the arrow-cut packs. The hands of the Apaches had been very full this day, but Usen had given them great riches.

. . . Many mules and horses, many bags of soccoro, Victorio enumerated.

Mangus Colorado remembered soccoro. All one summer bending his back for a few handfuls of corn, and here was full tribal harvest all in a day. Also he remembered the bags of corn piled in the plaza of Santa Rita.

Victorio continued:

"Many saddles and bridles and guns, many rolls of cloth, shawls, laces, shoes, tobacco in baled leaf, also tobacco hard-pressed and sweetened for the mouth. Canteens, knives, axes—all that go to fill shops of traders in Santa Rita—all the implements for 'cobre.'"

These last, it was agreed, might sink into the welter of sucking mud below (every hand's-breadth of moss cut and trampled into the black loam, not a lily standing on an unlopped stalk at sundown) but all other riches must be lifted from the marsh and cached high among the rocks, before the mud-covered bodies drove living men away.

Victorio saw the importance of this.

"Casks of mescal and vino; sacks of sugar and dried fruits—"

"*Ahai-ya-hiya-yip-pi!*"

Across on the slope the waiting Apaches were finishing one of the wounded. All day, hemmed in from either end of the canyon, the wounded Mexicans had tried to escape by climbing the slopes. One day had not sufficed to silence them all, but no one had escaped from the cienaga, so far; the rest could not.

"Sacks of white iron in coin—bottles of medicine, ointment that senoritas put on, and the thin black leggings without which they were never content—"

Mangus Colorado at last spoke:

"When the warpath is ended and all Mimbrenos gather in their own place, there will be time for feasting and all these riches will be opened, considered and well used."

Victorio bowed before him in the dark.

"Our people will then need great riches for the purchase of ninyas from the Mescaleros and the Chihuicahuis to make up for those lost at the feast of the plaza."

Victorio considered this a very forward-looking point.

"Time then for tuh-le-pah, vinto tinto, vino dulce. Even for mescal there will be time and place. Now, however, the time has not come."

The need for rigid abstinence was clearly seen by Victorio. His voice rumbled presently in the dark:

"Great war chief hold his thought over whole warpath of his people at one time. Little war chief Victorio hold his thought over Eagle Pass—"

"It is well spoken."

"Usen send great war chief to Mimbreno people. Mangus Colorado make all crooked trails straight."

"The hearts of the Mimbrenos will be very light, when they no longer burn to make answer for the feast in the plaza."

Their hands moved out, each taken by the other and crossed; allegiance made significant by the touching of loin and shoulder and temple.

Mangus Colorado now pondered a private matter. A clear cool impulse had shown itself for a moment in his mind: to leave the dun mare here until he came again or until Victorio and his warriors were called in; to spare her from the desert until her full recovery was assured. There was that in him which resisted this plan, however.

The cienaga would be closed for many weeks to all save creatures that fed upon death, so she could not stand there to be restored. Also the eye of another, even the eye of Victorio, is not like one's own in that which concerns a war pony, one of a thousand. His decision was against going without her, but the dun mare knew only the reata on that journey. He used two common ponies for his saddle and reached the Copper Mines, in less than two full days after his setting out.

XXXVII

Below in Santa Rita the miners and their women climbed the hill called the Needle* above the town. There they stood gazing into the southeast and then into the southwest. In the coverts above, the Apaches would shade their eyes and peer forward from their knees, now in one direction, now in another, then roll upon the gravel in silent laughter.

For Cuchillo Negro had sent in word of great destruction in Sonora including the extermination of a mighty conducta, at the cost of nine braves and fifteen wounded, a battle that all Sonora would remember. Moreover, his runners stated, many of his braves were now needed to guard the riches and herd the horses and mules, old men and boys in his command not being sufficient.

Thus Chihuahua flamed with terror under Victorio's stroke, and thus Sonora quivered under the dealing of Cuchillo Negro, but Santa Rita del Cobre continued to climb its hills to watch for the conductas. Nor was any word received in Santa Rita from Janos, for Coletto Amarillo was seeing singly, no drunkenness whatsoever in his eyes.

So the great silence fell upon Santa Rita; all was silence from the mountain and desert surrounding, and the little parties that hurried forth to see became a part of the silence. One day many miners were observed, not at their usual excavations, but in throwing rock and sand upon the shallow trenches, for the dead from the feast

---

*Now Kneeling Nun.

were restless. At night the coyotes uncovered them; over them the sky by day was cut with many circles.

One night a scout reported horses and mules being made ready in the plaza, "Los Go-dammies" at last intent upon departure and far richer than they came, each man now having a horse and saddle, also a mule or more for his belongings, where they had had but five worn mules between them at their coming. At daybreak they set out, not south to Janos nor by either pack-train route to old Mexico, but straight west toward the country of the Chihuicahuis.

Mangus Colorado had only waited to determine their direction to begin a big detour. Forty warriors were in his party, and these to a man had volunteered, for he had told them all would not return; that even he might not return. Wano-boono had perceived that the warpath of the Mimbrenos was crossed by death this day, but all agreed that law could never rightly be balanced if these whites were permitted to depart. A party of nearly-grown boys had asked to go, but he sent them back.

His men circled forward under cover of the hills, riding at double the pace of their quarry. They carried little water and less food; a few had flintlocks as well as bows—forty men and horses, the best of both at the old resort. Mangus Colorado had waited for this day. Until now the dun mare had been played with only. He carried the old rifle across his saddle; arrows and bow over his shoulder, at his belt the single-shot pistol which the white trapper had put to his mouth, a long knife in his right legging and a reserve knife under his breech-cloth. With the hills between them and the big game, he let out the mare and secretly exulted at the way she moved away from Indian ponies as if they were running to the knees in water. He raised his hand for silence as the murmur of admiration rose to the throats of the braves.

The fifteen whites were miles behind at noon and the Apaches had entered the Baked Lands, a great worthless stretch in the midst of the grass. After heavy rains the water lay here in broad thin sheets, its weight packing the clay hard. When the drouth followed, the clay dried and broke into thin tiles and then gradually powdered. Thus it lay now for many miles, lifting in spirals of yellow impalpable dust as the wind played, and completely enveloping any moving thing that traversed it. The whites were thus relied upon to furnish their own screen; otherwise the engagement would have been delayed until the foothills of the Chihuicahuis were entered. Withal, Mangus Colorado was apprehensive.

These were not Mexicans; nor were they Spaniards. Deadshots to the last man and heavily armed, with not only their lives but their riches in scalp money to protect. They were not to be attacked in a ravine pocket, nor suddenly to be awakened from sleep. These were the men who covered the fire-wagons in bags of corn, who posted themselves among Indian horses. The sight of them left Mangus Colorado less than himself; their laughter weakened his knees. He did not feel them contained in his thoughts as others were. Forty with arrows and a few practically untried guns were not more than equal to fifteen whose rifles were obedient to them as their eyes and hands.

Before mid-afternoon the distant dust-cloud told of the enemy entering the Baked Lands. Mangus Colorado adjusted his flexible force to fold about the point of the train. It had been necessary to leave his ponies at a distance, so that no sound of nickering would warn the oncoming band. Even so, water was sprinkled at the feet of the horses to keep the dust from rising above the gulch where they waited in concealment. On the distant Chihuicahuis signal smokes were rising, a calling together of warriors there. . . .

Coughing and cursing in the dust, "Los Go-dammies" entered the trap formed of two Apache lines. Mangus Colorado's eyes were foiled continually by the yellow dust-folds; once he glimpsed the face he searched for, but the screen closed again. His signal shot went into the mass instead of into the breast of "Senor Two Face" as he hoped.

The pack-train scattered, horses plunging, sending up curtains of dust. The Mimbrenos in full cry now emptied their guns, then sped their arrows. A high-pitched yell came out of the roiled mass—the favorite words of the Meh-hi-kanos and answering shots and the screaming of ponies. A bullet cut the air close to the lobe of Mangus Colorado's ear; beside him stretched a brave, biting at nothing, like a lizard pinned with thorn. Now he heard a high single shout and three horsemen spewed out of the mass, "Senor Two Face" in the lead, mouth open, eyes like balls of glaring white. It was not a charge, a trick possibly, but they seemed to be running away— "Senor Two Face" and two others yanking their mounts about and whipping them back toward Santa Rita.

Arrows sang into the blur from the length of the two Apache lines, but not one of the three whites was stopped. Mangus Colorado sent a shot at the long loose back, but it stayed upright in the saddle. Now with ten men, he was running for his horses, but the dust-cloud was distant before he reached them and began the chase.

He held the dun mare down from her top speed, continuing at the head of his company merely as fast as the slowest horse, yet he knew he could outdistance his warriors at will. Moreover, they knew this also, for he had foolishly permitted them to see the speed of the dun mare in the morning.

Of the two parties, his was the only mount held in. The Apaches slowly gained, holding the direction better through the dust of the Baked Lands. They were now entering the grass. One of the ponies ahead was thrown by a gopher hole. The rider tried to catch at the bridle of his nearest companion as he fell. His hand missed and the other did not stop. He scrambled up to one knee. The Mimbrenos curved about, sprawling him again with arrows, but his last pistol shot from the ground brought down a brave. Mangus Colorado signaled another to stay behind with the fallen and finish the white.

They were now in deep grama grass. The dun mare tugging at the bridle-rein at last found it loosened. From the saddle Mangus Colorado sent a shot after the leader ahead, but without result. He eased the empty piece into its boot and drew his bow. With a touch of the heel the mare closed farther in. At the hunched figure nearest he released an arrow and heard a groan. A second arrow sank beside it. The arms came up loose of bridle-rein, the body toppled backward. He circled it, dropping behind the mare's barrel, but there was no last shot from the ground this time.

Then he closed in on the long loose back. His first arrow missed. "Senor Two Face" bent forward whipping,

but the dun mare gained. A straight clear mark, but
another arrow sped wide. Two Face turned in the saddle
with rifle raised. Mangus Colorado pulled the mare
aside, ducking behind her at the shot. Her knees buckled;
she went limp in the air—from dead run to a long sliding
fall. Beside her, the chief was standing as his men
came up.

XXXVIII

H<small>E</small> <small>WAS</small> riding alone back toward the battle on the Baked Lands. The low sun was in his eyes, as he urged forward the fagged pony of the brave who had fallen out of the chase. He had little hope of the others who had kept on toward Santa Rita overtaking "Senor Two Face." His own arrows had curved about the enemy. The gods of evil loved and protected their own. The abhorred white-eye would again enter the presidio to breed plans that could not be foreseen. Moreover, the Nakai-yes would now begin to guess the nature of the silence that had fallen upon them. The peculiar shadow of this day persisted. Mexican soldiers might come out at the word of "Senor Two Face" to the relief of his party on the Baked Lands. . . .

The sickness he now felt in his body was not from the fall, nor from the fast fighting and trailing of the day. It was that he had not left the dun mare in the keeping of Victorio according to the clear cool impulse that had shown itself for a moment in his mind. Also he considered that a gift of Usen of greater speed than any other pony, can carry its rider into exclusive peril. Such a pony is therefore not for war but for the parades of peace, unless in the possession of a young warrior with his name still to make by one outstanding coup.

He now knew again the stiff sitting of a common horse, the droop of inert flesh when his whip relaxed.

Though the sun was merely a molten rim over the Chihuicahuis, firing still sounded from the dusty distance.

Seconds dragged between the shots—firing of a last stand, of a surviving few, now making each grain of powder count. Night had come when Mangus Colorado again took command. A dozen fallen Mimbrenos had been carried to the gulch where the horses were waiting, maddened with thirst. Five of those fallen were already packed for return to their people. Three whites at least were still alive in a breastworks of dead beasts and their packs.

Mangus Colorado sent back runners to Ponce for relief; also orders to watch Santa Rita for departure of Nakai-yi soldiers coming this way. He started back the dead and wounded, together with the animals of the whites' pack-train still upon their feet. With ten men left he held the noose. Before daybreak many of his people had come with water, food and many arrows; even squaws had stolen into the cordon before the light could show the dust of their approach. "Senor Two Face" had reached Santa Rita alive. Mangus Colorado now reflected on the one thing forgotten yesterday. Had he stationed a party in the grama grass, even the group of newly grown boys who asked to accompany him, "Senor Two Face" might have been headed off before Santa Rita was reached. Secretly he was ill-pleased with that day.

Morning broke with the Apaches crowding close. A circle of gunfire poured in at signal, followed by many arrows; and even then life moved behind the breastworks. Mangus Colorado became curious at last to see what manner of man was this last, who so stubbornly held out. His thought was to look into the face of that one while life still lingered in it. A brave was sent crawling forward with a lance carrying a white cloth.

The answer to offer of truce was a croaking laugh—words of a strange tongue, except the favorite words hoarsely shouted. An arm flung up as if in invitation—then silence.

They found him when the sun was high, opened by many wounds. No further wounds were made upon him by the Apaches, nor upon the bodies of his companions, for Mangus Colorado was convinced that these were brave men.

XXXIX

STILL the people of Santa Rita climbed their hill to look for the conductas.

Also no work was being done at the "cobre" diggings.

A point to be considered was that Santa Rita had not sent out Mexican soldiers for the relief of "Los Godammies" on the Baked Lands. Mangus Colorado thought at first that "Senor Two Face" might have been too badly wounded to lead the soldiers forth, but a scout reported seeing the white man in the street, walking alone and without laughter.

A party of fifty soldiers left Janos to relieve Santa Rita, and met Coletto Amarillo, who was powerful enough merely to harry and detain them until Apaches from Cuchillo Negro joined him. Then the Nakai-yes were driven back.

And still the people of Santa Rita climbed the hill, watching for relief.

A party of thirty miners and their families set out from Santa Rita for Janos—one-third of the people of the settlement. At the end of the first day's march, the Apaches, without attacking, showed themselves on two sides, and closed in at night to hear the prayers and wailings from the fireless camp. The Nakai-yes could not rest, but arose at midnight to fit their packs. At dawn Coletto Amarillo was ready in front and two Mimbreno wings, the left under Ponce, the right under Cuchillo Negro, and all in the hollow of Mangus Colorado's hand, closed in. Not until then was a shot fired. There was no face among those Nakai-yes that the Mimbreno chieftain cared to look upon with life remaining. He returned to his place and moved among the empty teepees above the Copper Mines.

Another night he stalked the settlement under cover of darkness. Such sounds as he heard were not of singing. The shops were closed; few lamps were lit. The street of the soldiers was in darkness. From one of the houses came a sound of mourning and a great fire was built in the yard, clothes and feathers piled upon it.

In this firelight the Medicine Padre moved, the people kneeling before him as aforetime. He then went to the mission, many following, and his voice sounded from the patio. It was not to the Virgin but to the Padre above him he raised his voice:

". . . . Strength, oh, Father—strength for thy people to meet the new grief . . . strength to bear our fear of the invisible eyes that are fixed upon us—"

Much was mere words, and the wind carried the voice from him at intervals, yet it was strength the Padre now asked for, not forgiveness.

". . . Strength for him whose people thy servant so blindly betrayed—that he may see the law above his law which he now so terribly invokes—

". . . Strength for him who lies—"

The murmuring of the people rose above the words of the Padre.

The trenches where the dead from the plaza had been carried were now ribbed high with rock and sand.

The next day the Mimbrenos watched the Nakai-yes carrying covered burdens to the open land dotted with white stones back of the mission. Three times the Padre walked with those who brought their dead. Formerly many days passed without one body being carried there. Wano-boono was consulted concerning this. Her eyes were dim so that there was no use for her to look down, but her lips muttered unforgotten words:

"*La viruela!*" and her hands came up to the ancient scars that pitted her skin. After a time Mangus Colorado said:

"It is then as if a battle were fought each day in Santa Rita."

"Each night, a battle also," said the old witch doctor. "Where hunger comes, comes *la viruela* feeding fast. Also where comes fear."

After that no scouts would go close to the village on account of disease.

At evening a last time came the Medicine Padre up-trail toward the old Mimbreno camp. His step was firm, his head uncovered. The white of it was like the whiteness of his face and the night was last to cover it. He reached the ridge and called the name of his friend:

"*Mangus Colorado—mi hermano!*"

He knelt and waited in silence, but there was no answer. Presently he arose as one without grief and spoke aloud:

"Even so, my brother, we shall meet again!"

Then he descended as he came.

XL

Tʜᴀᴛ ɴɪɢʜᴛ below in the plaza, activity of further departure was observed by the Apaches. At daybreak Mimbreno runners were sent to Cuchillo Negro, to Victorio, to Coletto Amarillo, for this was now seen as the long-awaited evacuation, not merely the passing of a portion. This was the day of all days since the taking of the warpath by the Mimbrenos.

In early forenoon men, women and children, all on foot since every available horse, mule and burro was burdened to capacity, strung out to the south and none turned southeast at the fork to Chihuahua. This was a concentration toward the presidio of Janos.

By noon that day every group, every figure of the flight had been studied by invisible eyes, but "Senor Two Face" was not perceived among them. Yet it had appeared that no living thing remained in Santa Rita. The slow drive continued through that day—and the next. Meanwhile Cuchillo Negro had again joined Coletto Amarillo; and Victorio drew near enough meanwhile to be drawn upon for reserve.

That, however, was no battle. It was the finishing of those already dead, an ending of misery for those already hopeless from hunger and thirst and paralyzed in their fears. In the midst of the dead and the dying, the Medicine Padre with a group of women and children about him, stood unscathed.

"These shall carry to Sonora and Chihuahua the full-

ness of our answer to the feast in the plaza," said Mangus
Colorado.

Thus were the books of the Mimbrenos balanced, yet
the heart of the leader burned to discover the last trick of
the hated White-Eye, for those who had watched pesti-
lential Santa Rita in the absence of the warriors reported
no movement there save of the birds circling lower.

XLI

THAT WHICH is done must be sung; that which is set
apart in several minds must finally be seen by all. Each
to his own part; this he sings, for he knows that best.
What the deed actually was is one thing; what it might
have been another. A measure of correlation is established
by talk; vanity is soothed. All Mimbrenos were bursting
to talk; the chieftain alone was silent.

Because Mangus Colorado was part of all actions; because each action lived first in his thought and transpired
according to his thought and not otherwise; because the
individual actions of all men keyed to his thought, and
he was present in the crisis of every action, nothing forgotten, all successful; because each man, in singing his
own deeds, sang also the thought of Mangus Colorado,
the chieftain himself could be silent.

Cuchillo Negro came in, driving great herds of horses
and cattle, even his saddle ponies heavy with packs. Still
another journey had then to be made to the secret
treasure-places beyond the Divide in Sonora, but other
men made this journey, for Cuchillo Negro now sat before Mangus Colorado telling what he had done. The
head men of all Mimbrenos were gathered to listen.

When two great men come together, the one who talks
most and is most eager to be understood is ever the
disciple, the master being him who has nothing to ex-
plain. And all can see this, save the disciple himself, or
one meshed in his own deeds. When at last Cuchillo
Negro ceased to speak of his deeds, it was seen that

Mangus Colorado was greatly concerned that others realize them fully. Thus Mangus Colorado spoke:

"When we sat waiting on the ridge above Santa Rita, the friend of my boyhood was already raiding the corrals of the enemy. While we feasted in the plaza, the dust of the warpath already filled his mouth. When our war parties were running out toward Janos, toward Chihuahua, our wounded crawling to Dark Canyons, the son of Soldado Fiero already held the enemy in Sonora in the cup of his two hands."

When the two great men stood at last after long sitting, those present to the last man perceived that the head of Cuchillo Negro came but to the armpit of Mangus Colorado, and thus his deeds stood also.

And Ponce came in, and Delgadito, and Coletto Amarillo, and lastly of all, driving great herds and supervising a caravan of treasure, came Victorio from Cienaga Alta and the Pass of the White Eagle. Even so, Victorio would not have tarried for the feast, but returned to his caches in the Mother Mountains for more riches, but Mangus Colorado sent those who were rested in his stead and still others to watch those who went first. Then to all head men he spoke of the night of his coming to Eagle Pass, and the order and the readiness of all that he found there, saying that he, Mangus Colorado, arriving in the camp of Victorio became as one suddenly rested without sleep. Also he told of the long fighting of the next day in the Womb of the Mother, and Victorio was risen to new stature.

Between these two there were conferences without witness. Victorio privately reported that during his waiting days in the Sierra Madre, he had found the bones of a Nakai-yi in one of the watered ravines, and nearby signs of yellow metal which the Nakai-yes valued above cobre, even above white iron. Mangus Colorado said he would look into this matter later. Between the chief and this lieutenant, deep understanding existed.

It was observed by others that when Mangus Colorado gave himself to the feasting and the drinking, Victorio refreshed himself with tuh-le-pah only and was wakeful; that when Victorio succumbed to the pleasures of the dance and the orgy, Mangus Colorado sat steaming in the hot caves, his mind ever following the scouts out-flung in all directions; relieving, replenishing, hearing their reports, extending his eyes and fingers thus to the very borders of the Mimbreno habitat in all directions.

Moreover, it was seen that a new Mimbreno law was not being tried merely, but already established: that for every man who feasted, another fasted, and for every man who lay drunken, another watched.

XLII

H AVING feasted among themselves, the Mimbrenos felt
the need to show their happiness to others. Runners were
sent with invitation to the chiefs of other tribes. From
the east, beyond the Big River came Gian-na-tah (Always
Ready), chief of the Mescaleros; and Piah from the north,
far beyond the Pinos Altos, hereditary chief of the White
Mountain people; from the northwest, Hash-kai-la of the
Coyoteros whose range bordered the sheep country of
the Navajos; from over the grama grass and the Baked
Lands came Shi-ka-she, the young chief of the Chihuicahuis; and from the southern *Ned-nis,* old Porico (White
Horse) with his face flattened from a youth. And with
each of these came sub-chiefs and the greatest of his tribe
in sorcery and singing and the telling of tales; also the
chosen of his women, the pride among his sons, and that
which was fit to show among his daughters.

All chiefs brought presents, each wondering what he
would take away; each sitting down to the feast silently
and reserving his words until such time as they rightly
warmed within him. For this was the day of testing
one another and the testing of strange liquors; unknown
fermentations and distillations of pack-trains that never
reached their destination. Pictured upon the bottles were
strange faces and fruits and ships, animals, devices of the
gods not vouchsafed to the Apache.

Some of these fabricos moving from hand to hand had
the bland taste of aloes; and some of the flavor of berries
forgotten since youth, and some of spices and others the

bitterness of herbs, but singularly and without exception the power of intoxication was noted in all. Taken together, the effects were even more curious, as early in the case of Hash-kai-la, who was led to the caves of steam. There his squaws worked over him, listening to words from his lips that had not found utterance in all his busy life hitherto. And that was before sundown and the high moment of the first day's feast, when a great basket was brought and lying in a circle of vine leaves was an unborn foal simmered golden in its natural jelly.

In the height of this delectation the voice of Cuchillo Negro was raised above other voices telling the life of Soldado Fiero, his father, from the beginning. And old Porico, whose face smiled eternally from the imprint of a horse-hoof that had flattened it, told how he had met Soldado Fiero before the climate changed, when they were ish-kay-nays together. One thing led to another in Porico's mind until one listening could not follow for the swiftness of his fancy. Then Porico's squaws came for him and one sat by, holding his nostril from the lip to ease the burden of his breathing.

And Cuchillo Negro was taken to his father.

For a while longer Gian-na-tah upheld the honor of the Mescaleros, until he was seized with trembling, and stared in front, head down like a *caballo loco* backed to the length of his reata. And a squaw went running to the nearest herd for warm mare's milk to return him to himself.

Then Piah told of feasts in the White Mountains (after conquest among the Maricopas) that had lasted nearly four times four days—from the night of the thin moon above the sunset to the fullness of the orb in mid-heavens.

But at that time, gently observed Piah, there were only tiz-win and tuh-le-pah, no inventions of the Nakai-yes to uproot the tall trees and change about the landmarks in a man's mind. Whereupon Piah's head fell upon his chest, though his spine stayed erect and unbending, for which he was famous.

Then Shi-ka-she of the Chihuicahuis and Mangus Colorado nodded across the remains of the feast. "And this," said Mangus Colorado, pointing to the great basket between them, "is the grama grass, and this jawbone, at the center, is the Baked Lands where 'Los Go-dammies' were fought in the dust. And where this Indian sits are the mountains of the Mimbrenos with the signal fires burning."

"Upon the peaks of the Chihuicahuis signal fires also burn in answer," said Shi-ka-she.

"The fires of the Mimbrenos say, 'Peace. You are welcome. Come to see us.'"

"And the fires of the Chihuicahuis say, 'We are coming.'"

They drank and wrestled together in exceeding amity and Shi-ka-she drew back the band of buckskin from his narrow temples for the night wind to cool his brow. When they could no longer talk, they made signs, and one would not sleep without the other so they slept together.

XLIII

THE MIMBRENOS had their lands again. They had not known what they lacked through the years; they had not known how the sun could come up over the mountains with the invader cast out. The sun wooed them like a lover; forgotten sweetness came back to the water springs and soundness to the earth. They climbed to the high places for the pleasure of looking in all directions over their lands.

Because they were vast roamers and rangers, the entire habitat remained fresh to them; none but the nomad knows the essential lure of his central council rocks. Tribal virtue was restored. In the rains of late summer, the Mimbreno heart also became green.

And all Mimbrenos knew that these things were, because a man had risen among them, and that these things were protected and fulfilled because his thought concerned itself with them continually.

There were no plots or jealousies, because this man had fulfilled his great stature with actions. There were none who approached him in height or strength or endurance, but his less obvious superiorities were also granted. It was not only what this man saw, but what he foresaw. Moreover, his people had seen him in the midst of other great chieftains and seen their thoughts bend to his, as cattle bend to the herder; seen them forget themselves to do him honor, and their secret delight when his eye settled upon them. They had heard the words of others, and his final word.

Usen, said Wano-boono, had chosen the Mimbrenos to send a pattern among them, the seed-man of a future people.

It was a time of great fulfillment. The old enemies of the Mimbrenos were conquered; the new enemies had not arrived. The thoughts of Mangus Colorado bulged over the borders and occupied themselves with the doings of other chiefs. When word came of old Piah's death, he sent runners to the White Mountain Apaches with word of the grief of all Mimbrenos; and gifts to his son, Kutu-hala. To Gian-na-tah he sent pinole and cattle when drouth destroyed the Mescalero herds. Of all the chiefs of Apacheria, Shi-ka-she of the Chihuicahuis, though ten years younger than himself, stood highest in his secret thoughts. And of all his own warriors, Victorio held his confidence more fully, though Cuchillo Negro stood second by hereditary right, and by the success of his annual raids in lower Sonora.

But Cuchillo Negro, ever the raider, was never the friend; words to the contrary through the years did not make it so. And Victorio, craftiest and surest of the Mimbreno soldiers, was a lieutenant only. He differed from Cuchillo Negro in knowing this and being content. in neither of these was Mangus Colorado met face to face. Standing thus alone he knew the loneliness of leadership, the isolation of the unrivalled.

Grass grew in Santa Rita after the rains. Grass covered the abandoned fire-wagons and cobre piles ready to be packed to the smelter; grass covered the open place dotted with white stones, even the plaza itself. Apache boys in venturesome packs that left nothing else untried, untouched, unsmelled, did not even approach Santa Rita in the fear of its curse, yet to Mangus Colorado there was unfinished business in that place. The one enemy of all Mimbreno enemies entered there and had not been seen to come out. The secret of the last trick of "Senor Two Face" was identified with the ghost of the town. . . .

As he remembered his enemy of all men, Mangus Colorado remembered his friend. Voices of men, nor the sounds of wind, water or tribal drums, could drown from his ears the voice of the Medicine Padre. From the years of listening long ago, words and snatches of meaning, not understood at the time, lived in his ponderings—seeds planted then, now meanings, prophecies, still unfolding. Of all the words of the Medicine Padre, his last as he stood upon the ridge of the empty teepees, after kneeling and calling the name, were most conned and remembered:

"Even so, my brother, we shall meet again."

Yet there was little hope of that. Medicine Padre was not in Janos. He had been very old when Santa Rita was abandoned by its people. There was little chance now that he even lived. Medicine Padre did not lie when he said that, yet the truth was difficult to discover. It was often so in the words of the Padre—a truth discovered afterward, from that which sounded as foolishness at the time.

It was so even in his talk of a "bridge."

XLIV

THE FIRST chill of the great shadow came from Gian-na-tah, chief of the Mescaleros. Far to the east, the Nakai-yes had engaged in battle with the whites, and a state of war existed between the two peoples. All Apache tribes connected up their lines of intelligence. From Kutu-hala of the White Mountain Apaches came word that the Nakai-yes far to the northeast were giving way before a huge army of Meh-hi-kanos—and that Mexican power was being broken throughout all that land, even from their long-established presidios. Though the Mexicans were permitted to stay, their allegiance was changed, it was said. Hereafter their eyes were forced to turn in obedience to great nan-tans of the Meh-hi-kanos, instead of to the Spaniards of the cities of the south.

So far, distant rumbling only; then the storm blackened and its direction became ominous to all Apacheria. Whites in countless numbers, not content to rest in the Mexican stronghold, called Santa Fe, had poured out on the march again, and were coming southwest. They marched slowly, covering each day less than half a sun's allotment of journey, but they did not stop, and their column stretched from mountain to mountain.

Mangus Colorado went forth to see. He traveled east to Big River and north along its valleys, establishing hidden camps behind him by which he could keep in touch with his own people; for it was not now possible for him to absent himself for a full moon like a warrior in the making. From the peaks of the Mazanos his eyes first fixed upon the new turn of his destiny.

First, Indian scouts stepping out in the lead (mischievous Pimas and Opatas), then white foot-soldiers all in blue alike, as many as all Mimbrenos standing together; then horse-soldiers, one like another, these, too, in prodigious numbers; great wagons with wheels high as a man and teepees on top; men with beards riding beside them, others driving the mules, sometimes four, sometimes six. White squaws in the wagon seats, and small ones. Between the wagons, sometimes small clumps of cattle were driven; many wagons piled with dried grass following—

The jaw of the watcher suddenly clicked: wonder and admiration sickened—

Fire wagons—five of them, and other wagons closed, in front and behind!

Mangus Colorado waited until all had passed, to the last laggard dust-raising foot; then made a hurried passage forward over pathless summits and defiles, to watch the parade all over again from the beginning.

This time he searched the monstrous human serpent for its Eye, the great nan-tan himself. That could not be the one—the beardless hat-wearer on a great horse among the tontos in the lead. Possibly in the circle of mighty horses that closely followed—riders in blue, curving around one who looked forward steadily, whose head was set upon a cushion of hair, no neck to speak of. . . .

Day by day they neared the land of the Mimbrenos; now east of the Pinos Altos, tramping the springs into mudholes, spreading out for game with shots and shouts— antelope and blacktailed deer in a fright that would last through the winter. The wagons could not come this way but followed the river to the south, a longer journey.

Meanwhile certain information had come to Mangus Colorado: that all the land north of the Apache country no longer belonged to the Nakai-yes, but to the Meh-hi-kanos; that the name of the great nan-tan was Kah-han-hee*; that he was so strong that he spoke merely and the result was the same as a battle which is won.

Thus he had spoken in Santa Fe, saying he was new governor and new medicine man and new war chief—saying that he came from his own chief of all Meh-hi-kanos to take over the lands of the Nakai-yes without disturbing the peace of those lands; that he came not to kill and steal; that to him the best man was the most peaceable man; that his soldiers would take nothing but what they paid for—

"Back of this nan-tan is another nan-tan still higher," repeated Mangus Colorado. He considered the point long. It was not so in the Mimbrenos. There was no chief above Mangus Colorado in all Apache tribes; but back of this nan-tan was one who did not even come out from his place to make war. The name of his place was Was-i-tona, and there were about him other whites, countless as the leaves of the trees, who did not come out for this war.

Mangus Colorado's head was bowed.

---

*Gen. Stephen W. Kearney.

XLV

CUCHILLO NEGRO counseled violence. He had watched
the wagon-train winding along the Big River, which was
now turned westward approaching Santa Rita. It was
very slow and clumsy; its accompaniment of soldiers not
large. The animals could be driven off; the women and
children put to death; Mimbreno warriors could vanish in
the mountains before the main body of whites arrived.

Mangus Colorado listened and spoke: "These are not
Nakai-yes. We are not at war with these people. We
will hear first what their nan-tan says."

"The Mimbreno made war against 'Los Go-dammies'
in times past," said Cuchillo Negro. "Of all our enemies,
there was none like him who lit the powder in the fire-
wagons—"

"That is true, but these are many and a strong people.
They have taken the lands of the Nakai-yes to the north
and the south. Their army has not stopped in many
days. It may not be in their minds to stop in the country
of the Mimbrenos."

"We do not permit strangers to pass through our
country—"

"It is true that they have not asked to pass, but they
are making war in their own way. It may be that they
have ways of making war which we do not understand—
like the fire-wagons hidden in the sacks of soccoro. Also
they have great numbers and many more behind them."

Mangus Colorado saw the sneer of Cuchillo Negro, the
same that was Pindah's and the same that he knew in

his own teepee before he had proved his right to bring
Aña in his own way, a sneer not seen in many years.

Now from their upper ridges the Mimbrenos saw lights
again in Santa Rita del Cobre, for of all the land surrounding, the Meh-hi-kanos chose the place of the dead
for their central camp, and those who could not crowd
in, pitched their tents close by, even on the ridges of rock
and sand where the dead from the plaza were taken.

That night Mangus Colorado slept little. The fear was
upon him that the Meh-hi-kanos had come to stay, and
many thoughts of heaviness beside. The next morning
he put on his eagle feathers and a fresh breech-cloth,
without which one is not dressed, the wide apron of it
hanging to his knees in front and behind, and new
moccasins and leggings to the thighs, and across his arm
a thin red blanket woven so tightly that it stood the rain
like deerskin—this from young Kutu-hala who had it
from the Navajos. Beside him was a rare present for the
great nan-tan—a bow fashioned of pieces of elk-horn
deftly fitted and bound together with sinew—a year in the
making by the master craftsman of the Commanches—
arrows of osage that lay winged and alive in the hand.

Then he sat down, waiting to be sent for, but no summons came that day. Mangus Colorado blamed the
Pimas and Opatas for not telling the nan-tan that he
had made his camp in the very center of the Mimbreno
hunting grounds. When he explained this, Cuchillo
Negro turned his back, one leg lifted, as Soldado Fiero
had done when the Nakai-yes had asked for his cattle
and horses.

And the second day no summons came, and the hills

about echoed with rifle shots for the white soldiers were hungry, so that even rabbits were welcome.

The third day a cheer roared forth from the village, for the wagons were sighted. The Apache runners brought word that their beasts were more dead than alive, having come through country that wheels never passed before and cut the corner of Jornado del Muerto on a day of customary heat. On that afternoon, two Opatas and four foot-soldiers came out from the village with a rifle upheld, to which a long knife was attached and on the end of that a cloth of white. Mangus Colorado sent a messenger to meet them. Word was brought back that their chief cared to see the chief of the Apaches.

Mangus Colorado replied:

"To great nan-tan say that the chief of Mimbrenos is ready. Say also that making talk in village of the dead is not good."

This word was returned, and after delay brought answer that the American general would come forth to the edge of the village. The shadows were long before all was ready on the slopes of the hill where the Nakai-yes had watched for their conductas. Last of all to come, walking with hurried steps was he whose head rested on his shoulders in the thick mat of his beard. His eyes glanced about, eye quick as a squirrel's, darting among the faces of Cuchillo Negro, Victorio, Ponce, Delgadito, Coletto Amarillo and fixing upon Mangus Colorado, not only for his central position and natural splendor, but as one chieftain picks out another. Full length Mangus Colorado felt his scanning eyes, but in his knees especially. Then Nan-tan Kah-han-hee spoke quick and low to one at his left hand who put his words into Spanish.

"The Army of the Americans does not come to make

war with the Indian. It does not come to kill or steal.
It is prepared to pay for that which it takes. Its present
need is mules—"

Mangus Colorado bowed and considered. At length he
said: "These are good words. Mimbreno people do not
rush to the warpath and think afterward. Mimbreno
people have watched the army of the Meh-hi-kanos crossing their land and put forth no hand against it. The
hand of the Mimbreno is now extended in friendship to
chief of the Meh-hi-kanos—"

His hand was quickly taken and as quickly dropped.
"In token of his friendship, the Mimbreno brings to the
great nan-tan a bow of elkhorn and arrows of osage—"

Mangus Colorado now presented his gift with admoni-
tion that it was better for the trophy-lodge than the hunt,
as rain would work evil upon the binding of the bow.
The interpreter passed the gift to the General, who
brought it to his eyes with a nod and passed it to one
behind him with thick-writing in his hands. Nan-tan
Kah-han-hee then spoke crisply again and was inter-
preted:

"The General thanks you for the gift and wishes to
inquire if his Indian friend has any mules."

Mangus Colorado did not appear fully to register this.

"Word has reached the Mimbrenos that the Army of
the Meh-hi-kanos comes to bring war against the Nakai-
yes," he said.

"Yes—" with a quick question that neither asked nor
answered, full into Mangus Colorado's eyes before he had
time to draw them into himself.

Mangus Colorado bowed and pursued:

"My people have beaten the Nakai-yes many times and

are still at war against them. The Nakai-yes would not
dare to cross the lands of the Mimbreno. The Nakai-yes
are truce-killers. They are no good north or south. Now
Meh-hi-kanos come to make war with Nakai-yes. That
is good. Mimbreno people and Meh-hi-kanos join hands.
Soon Nakai-yes be no more. Then Mimbrenos and Meh-
hi-kanos make long peace all time together."

The face of Nan-tan Kah-han-hee did not light with
joy when the interpreter conveyed this. His answer was
again brief.

"The Americans do not need help to fight the Nakai-
yes, but they do need mules."

Mangus Colorado did not answer. His face betrayed
nothing of what was passing in his mind. More words
were conveyed to him—that to continue their journey into
the west the white man needed mules; that they still
had far to go; that they were ready to trade mules or
purchase mules; that thirty mules would be providential
and fifty a godsend.

When all was said, Mangus Colorado drew back a step
and turned his eyes up-trail. He pointed to the sunset
and then across to the east. "Another sun, my warriors
will bring mules to the wagon-train of the Meh-hi-kanos,"
he declared and departed.

XLVI

THE WHITE man's army pushed westward across the grama grass toward the Chihuicahuis, leaving a great scar like that of the cougar's claws across the face of Wanoboono. A scar was left with Mangus Colorado also, but different in two ways. It did not show and it did not heal.

The Mimbrenos had their lands again, nothing outwardly changed. Many thought the curse that had hung over Santa Rita had gone to the whites and departed with them, for the ruined village was not so completely shunned as aforetime by the Apaches. It was discussed for a time that Mangus Colorado had given whole mules for broken ones; and that his offer of allegiance to the white nan-tan was not importantly considered, but even the murmuring of Cuchillo Negro died down.

Only Mangus Colorado remembered. He had felt the evil wind of the future blowing across his country. What had happened once could happen again. He had seen Nan-tan Kah-han-hee, but the nan-tan had not seen him as differing from another Indian. Back of Nan-tan Kah-han-hee was another nan-tan—

One day Mangus Colorado looked about his own teepees at the Warm Springs. Three daughters of Aña were growing up and in a way all their own. The oldest was ready to put her bells on. Many young fanciers, including sons of Cuchillo Negro, had seen her and were eager to fasten their ponies at her mother's teepee, but her readiness had not been announced. She was called Sons-nah,

Corn Tassel, and knew her own value, but in a way that did not make her hated. She could come to her father with a boldness Aña had never learned, yet making her father like it. The massacre of Mimbreno women and girls in the plaza had subtly worked to enhance the value of those that remained; none knew this apparently so well as Sons-nah.

She came forward now, eyes big like her mother's, but without the fear; little purses filling in her breast and the waist of one not yet learned in the full value of food. Her movements called the eye; only the squaws were indifferent to it. Her mouth had not been cut with a knife. Her step said, "Look at me."

Mangus Colorado watched under his great brows. His eyes told nothing, but his brain knew that the world was moving on. Her mother had not been like this, but the blood of the Apache had become quick in her first child. All that one has done lives again. . . .

There had been a thatch of willows and days in the checkered light of alder branches, as he lay cut and bleeding from the knife of Lost Pony. (Aña's hands had trembled as she served, Aña's heart beating like the heart of the dun mare at the end of her run across Jornado del Muerto). And this one had not the fear of the mother, nor the will of the father, yet each lived again in her and something of her own besides.

Mangus Colorado spoke what was in his mind and Aña wept, but that was to be expected. Aña's mother had wept also. From the trophy lodge, they drew out the finest garments and from the corral of woven ocotillo the flashiest ponies. Aña followed them to the end of the hills; then her eyes followed them after that across the grama grass—Mangus Colorado riding ahead, young Mangus, son of Placid now fourteen, slightly behind at his left, and third, Corn Tassel often looking back.

Beyond the Baked Lands, riders of the Chihuicahuis met them with greeting and led the way. They passed through lanes of warriors and women, pointing on and up, always higher, until the cedars were far apart and live oaks squatted in stature and only the lodge-pole pines flourished, to the end of the timber-line—on and up to the inner stronghold of the Chihuicahuis where Shi-ka-she stood in welcome. . . .

When night had come and the central fire blazed at the kan-gan-hay before the lodge of Shi-ka-she, and the beating of the esada-dedne had become a part of the rhythm of the night, the two chiefs sat together with others about them, but not too near.

They talked of the Meh-hi-kanos. Shi-ka-she had seen them passing and on to the distant westward. He had not seen Nan-tan Kah-han-hee close at hand, but he had seen others. There was one called Keet Kah-sohn held very high among the whites whom he had seen close at hand. Keet Kah-sohn* made great passages alone across the country of many tribes, carrying messages from the Great Father in Was-i-tona. No Indian molested Keet Kah-sohn, for he knew their ways and many chiefs were known to him. Meh-hi-kanos were many, but few were like Keet Kah-sohn, who kept his word, Shi-ka-she said, even when made at daybreak after double-seeing comes from mescal. A great friend of the Indian, from whom Indian chiefs could learn many things for the good of their people—and how white men could be approached.

---

*Kit Carson.

White men could think fast, yet remain cool, Shi-ka-she said, but one thing they followed without reason, that was pesh-klitso, yellow iron. For that they went loco, one and all. He had the word of Keet Kah-sohn on this also.

Mangus Colorado secretly longed for such a friend among white men to make devious matters straight in his thoughts. Finally after many words that which concerned his present coming was leisurely opened:

"This," said Mangus Colorado indicating Placid's son, "this ish-kay-nay has long been of no account in the camp of the Mimbrenos. The great rains do not wet him; horses do not kill him; the wisest of our medicine lodges do not make him astonished—"

He caught up a little coal and tucked it into the fold of leaf-bound tobacco and filled his great lungs.

"The same," he resumed, "even fire-wagons covered in corn sacks could make no more present, for on that day, with bone and flesh all parted about him, it was he and no other who pushed himself up from the ground, using his feet and hands also, as one who would not be left with the dead. In the camp of my friend for a time, some value may be found in him—"

"The sons of one's women are one thing," said Shi-ka-she, "but the son of one's friend is another."

"And that," Mangus Colorado pointed to Corn Tassel sitting just so among the ninyas of the Chihuicahuis where firelight and shadow wrestled together. "That, of the first labor of her mother, the Nakai-yi, by some medicine which I myself have forgotten, is restless in the thoughts of many young men. To give her to one would make all others angry. To divide her among them would do for a slave only. Also the ignorance of young men in matters pertaining to ninyas is clearly understood—"

Shi-ka-she nodded gravely.

"And old men are alive in their heads and not else-where—"

Again Shi-ka-she nodded.

"To my friend therefore who is neither old nor young, I come for counsel—"

Shi-ka-she turned from the fire and gazed through the dark to the east. "In the days of my father's rulership of his people, the camp of the Mimbrenos at the Warm Springs was far, oh, very far away (ah-han-day—ah-han-da-ay!). Now the council rocks of the two peoples are close at hand, the signal fires blaze together. The heart of Shi-ka-she burns warmly at the gift. The back of this ninya shall not be bent with heavy burdens nor her hands knotted with labor. Though a squaw only, the blood in her veins shall always be remembered by Shi-ka-she as the presence of the great brother himself."

"It is well," said Mangus Colorado.

The second daughter of Aña was sent to Kutu-hala of the White Mountain Apaches, and later the third to Co-si-to, the son of Hash-kai-la of the Coyoteros. Thus Mangus Colorado ensconsed centers of himself in high places over all Apacheria, a transfusion of his own blood in other tribes. Thus the Mimbrenos came to hear of him from across their borders, and the lips of strangers greatly magnified his name among themselves. And still, though he bridged all barriers among the Apaches, and was chief among chieftains of all lower Athapascan peoples, he continued darkly to ponder on the great nan-tan back of the

Nan-tan Kah-han-hee, and of those countless as the leaves of the trees, who had not yet found the way to the land of his people. Such ponderings on the nature of the white men made simple his rulership over the red, as ponderings upon the nature of women make simple the ways of men.

XLVII

CUCHILLO NEGRO was beside himself. Not only was a big party of white soldiers on the way to the Copper Mines, but he had been insulted by one who rode far ahead on a great black horse—one who could not bend forward in the saddle for the guns and knives in his belt— one who claimed to be Meh-hi-kano but talked Spanish so freely that he could jeer at the Mimbrenos for not keeping a better watch on their country, as well as to make clear his message.

Cuchillo Negro's Spanish was meagre, but what he had not understood from words he had seen with his two eyes. More trouble, very great trouble had fallen again on the Mimbrenos. Mangus Colorado listened until the whole story was drawn out.

It was winter; a thin blanket of snow was on the ground. Cuchillo Negro had been hunting with twenty-five braves beyond the Big River two suns east of the Copper Mines, in a thickly wooded country of game, when the solitary horseman appeared. This stranger had two short guns at his belt, two more in holsters, a rifle across his knees, also a long and a short knife. He advanced leisurely, making a whistling sound like a cooch-wundah (wood chuck). Many of the trees had dropped their leaves so that ambush was difficult, yet he came into the net made for him, and might have been shot from the saddle save that Cuchillo Negro cared to talk with him first and perhaps prolong his passing for women and children to enjoy.

At a signal the stranger was halted, the warriors rising

from covert about him. In no way stampeded, he glanced about from face to face. Cuchillo Negro approached in front, but was stopped by Spanish words: "Estamos amigos (we are friends) but not too close, Senor, or I will shoot!"

Such words angered Cuchillo Negro. He replied that if he had not wished for talk, the body of the white man would even now be cooling on the snow. At this the stranger laughed, saying that to kill him would be the worst day's work the Apache ever did; that his friends in large numbers were following close behind. Furthermore he said that while his friends had not come for war, they were prepared for it. Cuchillo Negro did not believe this. He told the stranger that his talk was foolish, that if he belonged to a big party, he would not have left it, to advance so far alone. Again the white man laughed and his answer this time was very bold:

"Indian—you don't know your own business. Your young men have been asleep. Your squaws have kept them in camp when they should have been on the watch. Look—"

On a distant ridge the eyes of the Mimbrenos then opened to a long line of soldiers in coats to their knees, with glistening tubes in their hands.

The iron-belted one, so sure in authority and unmindful of peril, was left sitting on his horse. Cuchillo Negro thereafter said no more, but hurried to Mangus Colorado with word. No time was to be lost, he now advised. In two days the Meh-hi-kanos would be here, if not exterminated in the ravines of the Sierro Caballo or in their crossing of the Big River—

To the added disgust of Cuchillo Negro, Mangus Colorado did not accept this as an instant call to war.

He put his people in readiness, however, and went to look for himself. As he traveled, he reflected much on the words of the iron-belted one to Cuchillo Negro—words and fearless laughter, even taunting the Mimbreno for having been caught off his guard. It was true. Four winters had passed since the departure of Nan-tan Kah-han-hee, and the Apache had fallen asleep with another army visible on his ridges.

But, thought Mangus Colorado, how could the white stranger have known this, and at a moment when his own life was like a small bird in the hands of a boy?

Sickness closed upon him as he watched the second white invasion fording the Rio Grande—sickness that was never fully absent, but sometimes like now, becoming acute to the very knees. "Estamos amigos," he muttered as the column pressed the current among the snow-whited stones that made the water black in its running.

Unless this were merely an advance guard, it was by no means so great an army as Nan-tan Kah-han-hee's. Many burdened mules, but no wagon-train visible, no fire-wagons. One single carreta, however. This was like no wagon ever seen before, but covered in black, fashioned and adorned with much labor, the horses spirited, and this for men to ride in only and not their packs. Those within were not dressed as soldiers.

Now the chill of the day entered the bare knees of Mangus Colorado, causing them to tremble, for the great thought seized him that this was the coming of the Great White Father himself, the nan-tan back of Nan-tan Kah-han-hee from far off Was-i-tona, the abode of thousands. Perhaps he who had laughed at Cuchillo Negro—the one stiff at the waist with iron arms—was the Great One; or one of those sitting in the carreta—

XLVIII

Unerringly to the ruins of Santa Rita the column moved, soldiers filing into the presidio, the others taking possession of the 'dobe houses, clearing the buildings and streets, raising tents, driving their herds to winter-killed grass. This time Mangus Colorado was not held in waiting three days, but summoned at once.

At the foot of the slope to the village he saw the chiefs gathering to meet him. Among them was the chief of the soldiers, also the one who had taunted Cuchillo Negro, and another to whom all now looked—one of those who had crossed the Big River in the carreta— darkly dressed and without ornament. Seen close at hand, this one proved different from all men, in that he not only looked through his eyes, but through eyes of glass in front of them. Especially soft from long sitting, was this one, and it was he who spoke, his hand now extended, fingers soft as udders in the clasp of Mangus Colorado. He made no sound of laughter in speaking, yet marks of laughter remained on his face. When he ceased to speak, lo, it was Iron Belt,* the taunter of Cuchillo Negro, who put his words into Spanish:

"We have heard the name of the great chief, Mangus Colorado. We have also read the report of General Kearney of his passing through this country and of securing mules at a time of great need. We come to tarry with our Indian friends for a little while until a certain

---

*Captain Cremony, official interpreter for the Bartlett Boundary Commission, later known for his book "Life Among the Apaches."

work is accomplished. We come in peace. We mean
to dwell in peace with the great chief and all his people.
We hope to depart in peace, wiser as to one another and
warmer in friendship."

"It is well," said Mangus Colorado. Presently he inquired if this coming had to do with war-making upon
the Nakai-yes. Nan-tan Four Eyes shook his head and
told Iron Belt to say:

"There is no war whatsoever in the thought of this
coming—neither to the Indian nor the Mexican. The
Great Father of our country has made peace with the
Mexican people, and the work which he has sent us to
do concerns that peace—the establishing for all time the
exact boundary between the two nations. The lines are
to be made straight that peace may endure."

Not the Great White Chief from Was-i-tona—merely
another of his servants sent forth with an army to protect
him and his work; and Iron Belt brave enough alone to
laugh at Cuchillo Negro and twenty-five Apaches—an
interpreter merely! Mangus Colorado did not feel ready
for further pow-wow, without having time to consider
affairs so extraordinary. He could not depart abruptly,
however, and saw no harm to inquire how long Nan-tan
Four Eyes meant to stay. This was not known, but
some weeks at least would be necessary. Mangus Colorado pointed out that the preparations for camp in Santa
Rita appeared very extensive and far-reaching.

"It is the custom of our country thoroughly to police
and prepare a camping site, and to roof such buildings
as we find, even though we remain but a little time,"
the Meh-hi-kanos said.

The Nakai-yes had made no such sound of hammers

in the beginning even though they planned to stay always. Mangus Colorado departed, saying that he would consider all that had passed between them and come again after further pondering. . . .

There was much to consider, much to learn. The American party numbered three hundred—four-fifths of which were soldiers, but the leader of the soldiers was always second in command to Nan-tan Four Eyes* whose name and title were not to be mastered easily in a day. Iron Belt was also a matter of confusion. Apparently he was of the soldiers as well as of those who were not concerned in war.

It was important that the name of Mangus Colorado had gone abroad even to the Great Father himself and that Nan-tan Kah-han-hee had set down this name in his thick-writing. One could not have thought that Nan-tan Kah-han-hee was concerned with other than mules. The name of Mangus Colorado had not gone abroad, however, as conqueror of the Nakai-yes and as war lord of all Apaches; at least, it did not properly deter the Meh-hi-kanos from entering the country of the Mimbrenos without asking and when they wished.

Nan-tan Four Eyes was also much concerned with thick-writing.

Another matter of profound import: No mescal whatsoever was to be had in the camp of the Meh-hi-kanos. This was hard to believe. Even in the partaking of food, there was no mescal, or vinos even, nor was there pleasure in asking. Moreover, the name "Los Go-dammies" was without pleasure to the ears of these Meh-hi-kanos. It was not the name by which they were known in the

---

*John R. Bartlett, U. S. Boundary Commissioner, 1850-53.

country of Was-i-tona, Nan-tan Four Eyes said, nor even the name of a tribe.

Still another: One day in Santa Rita, Iron Belt asked to see the short gun of Mangus Colorado. He took it in his hand and made laughter about it, saying it had the narrow chest. He then said, "Look at me, Mangus Colorado," drawing a pistol from his holster, and firing six times without once stopping to reload. Mangus Colorado's head was bowed as he walked up-trail to his own place that day, for all the horse-soldiers of the Meh-hi-kanos had guns like this, and each man was as six men with that one short piece.

Still these people did not care to make war. They even called the Nakai-yes "brothers" and were inclined at this time to protect them. The people of Chawn clizzay were one kind; the people of Senor Two Face, another; the soldiers of Nan-tan Kah-han-hee were one thing; the people of Nan-tan Four Eyes still another. All Meh-hi-kanos, but exceedingly various and past finding out. One's need for a true friend among them was very great.

Of them all, Nan-tan Four Eyes talked most of friendship, and his actions were according. Mimbrenos were made welcome when they ventured into Santa Rita; and he, Mangus Colorado, was frequently sent for, when he did not go of his own accord. Food was spread on high boards. One had to watch carefully, since the eating of the Apache was not like this; one had to watch so carefully that one did not know he had eaten afterward. These people ate neither horse nor mule, but bear was often brought in from the mountains, and made ready among other flesh, so it became necessary to point to the plates asking, "Is this bear meat—or that?" since no

Apache would eat the flesh of the wise brother. All
would then laugh saying which was bear and which was
not, but the closed fires of the white men worked strange-
ly upon all meats, leaving them in such shapes and savors
that one could not be sure. There came a day when Iron
Belt said:

"Mangus Colorado, you are to have a great present, so
that you will soon be taking the white man's road."

One then came with a marked string in his hands,
and a breech-cloth worn on the outside instead of next
to the skin, and Mangus Colorado leaped up at the touch
of his hands and became mightily afraid his time had
come, for this one began to go over him with the string—
around his loins and shoulders and chest, straightening
out his limbs in unknown medicine. That was all of that
for four days, when Mangus Colorado was sent for and
the man with the string was present, but this time he
had with him a great dress of blue cloth and buttons of
yellow iron. Mangus Colorado would have taken it
away to his own teepee, but Iron Belt said it was the
pleasure of Nan-tan Four Eyes to see his present worn.
So alone with the man of the string he put it on, piece
by piece, being advised at all points, some of which were
not to his liking. However, the pleasure of others was
very great, and Iron Belt said:

"Now, Mangus Colorado, you have taken the white
man's road."

Apart at his own teepees the present was closely examined, first by his own women and children; then for
three days others came to see and hold it in their hands
and to their faces. Since the days of his name-making
and finding the shirt of red wool in the cache of Chawn
clizzay—nothing had happened to bring such grandeur

to his person in the eyes of all Mimbrenos. But Mangus Colorado did not entrust to his own people the words that went with the present—that by this he was taking the white man's road.

Soon afterward he went down into Santa Rita del Cobre, wearing the great gift. This time, however, he did not tuck the shirt inside of his pants so hotly; that was asking too much. Iron Belt did not come to meet him as usual this day, and the first that he saw was one with blackened face, putting iron shoes upon a horse, and this man opened his mouth and laughed; then teamsters at the corral took up the laugh and soldiers hurriedly gathered, making a great noise until Santa Rita was intent upon this one thing and no other—

Then Nan-tan Four Eyes came running forward and all grew instantly silent. Many words in the strange tongue were then spoken, but Mangus Colorado did not answer, for the heat in his brain made words uncertain and the blood in his eyeballs made the face of the nan-tan before him a thing fit for death only.

Farther than ever before that day was the white man's road from the urge of his steps.

XLIX

Cuchillo Negro sulked in his teepee. There were others who said all this had happened before; others who pointed significantly to the fire-wagons of the Nakai-yes still in the plaza of Santa Rita. But these were not in authority and Mangus Colorado continued to hold his people in a state of friendliness toward the whites.

The Americans did not rightly attend to the grazing of their animals, many straying to mix with the Apache herds. It was not easy to account for all those, and the temptation to drive off a few mules for a feast was strong among the young men of the Mimbrenos. Repeatedly, however, Mangus Colorado restrained them, and made it a matter very desirable for them to return the straying animals to the Americans. Nan-tan Four Eyes approved of the care of Mangus Colorado in this matter.

One day two Mexican boys, prisoners of a raid years ago in Sonora, accompanied the warrior who owned them for a visit to Santa Rita. While there, the two boys ran suddenly to the tent of Iron Belt demanding protection. The Mimbreno followed, asking for them, but Iron Belt took them to Nan-tan Four Eyes who would not give them up.

On that day word also had come to Mangus Colorado of another body of white men coming into the Pinos Altos, to scratch the rocks for yellow iron. This was a matter of grave concern and he left with Victorio for a look at the miners. The following day, however, he presented himself with his sub-chiefs in Santa Rita and asked for the return of the prisoners of the Apaches. Nan-tan Four Eyes shook his head, saying this could not be.

"Why do you take our captives from us?" asked Mangus Colorado.

"Because they came to us and demanded our protection."

Mangus Colorado then spoke once and for all that day:

"You came to our country. You were well received. Your lives, your property, your animals were safe. You passed by ones, by twos, by threes through our country. You went and came in peace. Your strayed animals were always brought home to you again. Our women and children came here and visited your houses. We were friends—we were brothers! Believing this, we came among you and brought our captives, relying on it that we were brothers and that you would feel as we feel. We concealed nothing. We came not secretly nor in the night. We came in open day and before your faces, and showed our captives to you. We believed your assurances of friendship, and we trusted them. Why did you take our captives from us?"*

"We do not tell lies," said Nan-tan Four Eyes. "The greatness and dignity of our nation forbids us doing so mean a thing. Four years ago we were at war with the Mexicans, but that war is over. The Mexicans are now our friends and by the terms of this peace we are bound to protect them. We know you have not ceased your hostility against Mexico, but these captives are Mexicans whom we are bound to protect. We will send them to their country and set them at liberty there. We cannot lie."

---

*Transcription of Magnus Colorado's speech and other talk quoted in this chapter is from Bartlett's Personal Narrative, 1856.

Mangus Colorado sat unmoved through this delivery by Iron Belt. When it was over, he made no sign of rising. Ponce, however, excitedly arose, saying: "But these are our prisoners. They were made in lawful warfare. You took them from us without warning—" his temper was getting away from him and Iron Belt signalled him to stop.

"Our brother speaks in anger," he said. "Boys and squaws lose their temper, but men reflect and argue—"

"I am neither a boy nor squaw. I am a man and a brave. I speak with reflection. I speak of wrongs done upon us by the Nakai-yes and of wrongs you do us now—" again Ponce was wrathfully gesticulating, and Iron Belt took him by the shoulders and pressed him down. The white men looked to Mangus Colorado, but he made no sign.

Nan-tan Four Eyes then explained that he took the prisoners in pursuance of orders of the Great Father in Washington whose word was, "You must take all Mexican captives you meet among the Apaches and set them at liberty." While there was no disobeying the orders of the Great Father and it was not the custom of Americans to buy prisoners, he said that there was a Mexican in his employ who might buy them. If he had not the money, the Americans would loan it to him.

Delgadito arose and said, "The brave who owns these captives does not want to sell. He has had one of these boys six years. His heart-strings are bound around him. He is as a son to his old age. Money cannot buy affection. His heart cannot be sold. He taught him to string the bow and wield the lance. He loves the boy and cannot sell him."

Nan-tan Four Eyes: "We are sorry that this thing should be. We feel for our Apache brother, and would like to lighten his heart. But our brother has fixed his affection on the child of his enemy, and our duty is stern. It wounds our hearts to hurt our friends; but if they were our own children, and the duty of the law said: 'Part with them,' part with them we would. Let our Apache brother reflect and name his price."

Talk then ended. The Apaches conferred and agreed to accept "calicoes, blankets and sheetings" from the American commissary for the prisoners, but the subject-matter was not forgotten.

L

ONE DAY soon afterward Nan-tan Four Eyes sent for
Mangus Colorado and they blew a cloud together before
speech. On the table before the Meh-hi-kanos was a thin
slab of wood with black marks on it.

"Senor Commissioner would like to know if you ever
heard of a white man here at the Copper Mines named
Johnson?" Iron Belt began.

Mangus Colorado made a pretense of arranging the
blanket on his arm, though his heart had leaped within
him; "Senor John-sohn—Senor Two Face!" he said.

He was pressed for explanation. Turning his eyes to
the old rusty howitzers in the plaza, he told the story of
the Soccoro massacre. When he had finished, Nan-tan
Four Eyes said:

"Mangus Colorado, your people have suffered great
wrongs from the Nakai-yes. Also from that man—mis-
called an American—for whom all other Americans must
suffer as well—"

"Senor John-sohn—how you know him?"

Iron Belt took in his hand the old slab of wood. "This
was found by one of my men in the place of Mexican
graves. This writing tells us of one Johnson, first name
not known, an English or American fur-trapper, who
died and was buried here many years ago."

"Black writing say how he die?" asked Mangus Colorado.

"Yes—*la viruela.*"

"Huh."

"And what you have told us makes us understand this line below:

'May God have mercy on his soul for the great
wrong he committed in our midst.—Font Fr.'"

Mangus Colorado stood upon his feet and pressed his moccasins firmly on the hard-tramped floor of turf and strode out.

LI

I T WAS now summer. The Meh-hi-kanos had occupied
the Copper Mines six months. Mangus Colorado had not
found the friend he sought in any of the Meh-hi-kanos.
Iron Belt was full of strange devices. He asked many
questions for each one he answered. He not only knew
Spanish, but had learned many Apache words, and
practiced on all who came near, yet there was that about
Iron Belt that made the Indian feel his nakedness, and
to sit in anger long afterward alone in his teepee.

Nan-tan Four Eyes was busy with his boundary matters
and his thick-writing; the nan-tan of the soldiers was a
brave man, but set himself apart. Those who went near
him of his own men put their heels together and made
the sign of a clean heart before speaking. The soldiers
themselves were beneath consideration, all being alike and
kept so, sleeping and eating at one time. There was not
among the Meh-hi-kanos one like Keet Kah-sohn, whom
Shi-ka-she had sat with, whose word stood upright until
what he said was unspoken, having been fulfilled.

Still Mangus Colorado managed to keep all Mimbrenos
impressed with the importance of remaining friendly and
patient with the interlopers and there was no dangerous
outbreak of ill feeling until the day a shot crashed in the
plaza and a party of Apaches there stampeded to the hills
with the horrible image of the "soccoro" massacre before
their eyes. The nan-tan of the white soldiers followed
after them holding up his hand—Iron Belt behind him

and still farther, Nan-tan Four Eyes—all beckoning the Apaches to come back.

"We are friends. The one who fired the shot is taken prisoner and full justice will be done," called Iron Belt when the Apaches permitted him to come up.

At the word of Mangus Colorado, the Mimbrenos consented to go back. A Mexican teamster name Jesus Lopez in the employ of the boundary people had shot an Apache; the latter seemed to be dying. A cook had seen the altercation; there was no palliation. The Indian was unarmed. Lopez was put in chains and thus shown to the Mimbrenos. Days passed, the Indian fighting for life. He was not given to his people, but cared for in the hospital of the Meh-hi-kanos. After a month of miserable suffering his life flickered out. The Apaches refused a coffin for him, put his body on a horse and took him to the hills. Then they came back, asking that the murderer be delivered into their hands. Nan-tan Four Eyes expressed himself unable to comply.

"We utterly regret that this thing has happened," he said. "One Mexican endangers all our efforts toward peace together, but our laws cannot be changed. It is not in our power to punish this offender. There is above us, not only the Great Father in Washington but a high chief in Santa Fe, governor of all this territory, who alone has the power to administer justice to this unfortunate man. To this great chief, I will send the murderer of our Apache brother. This is all I can do regarding him, but to the family of the dead warrior we are prepared to pay a sum in blankets or cotton cloth or corn, or money, if you prefer—"

Mangus Colorado declined to speak. Ponce arose:

"Senor Commissioner speaks well. He has not the double tongue, but would money satisfy a Meh-hi-kano for the death of his brother? Would money pay a mother for the death of her son? Money will not bury our grief. Money will not pay this mother for our dead brave. She wants no goods. She wants no corn. She wants the life of the murderer. For that she is willing to die herself. Without that she is unwilling to live."

Nan-tan Four Eyes answered:

"You speak with the heart of feeling. I feel as you do. All Americans feel as you do. Our hearts are sad at your loss. I know that money or goods cannot pay for your loss, but it will be well for the women and children of the dead brave to have food and blankets when winter comes. All that we can do in that way will be done, but we cannot give the murderer into your hands. He must be taken to Santa Fe for trial. The Governor alone has the right to administer the punishment to Jesus Lopez."

Mangus Colorado arose and gravely said:

"I cannot answer for my people if this thing is done. My people are ruled by law, not by words of mine or any chief. Our laws also cannot be changed. My people will not be satisfied to hear that the murderer is punished in Santa Fe, they want him punished here where they can see him die. Then my people will know that the Meh-hi-kano brothers do justice by them."

"This is impossible to grant, Mangus Colorado. We respect you. We thank you for your treatment of us in all the time we have been here. We appreciate how steadily you have caused to be brought back our straying horses and mules, how staunchly you have stood between us and some of your people who felt aggrieved over our sending the Mexican boys, your former prisoners, back to their country. We even see your side of this miserable affair, but our hands are tied. . . . Still, you are chief of all your people, and we must hold you responsible for them. If our animals stray, we shall call on you to find them and bring them back, as you have done. While the Apaches continue to do this, the Americans will be their friends and their brothers. But if the Apaches take our property and do not restore it, they can no longer be the friends of the Americans. War will then follow; thousands of soldiers will take possession of your lands, your grazing valleys, and your watering places. They will destroy every Apache warrior they find, and take your women and children captives."

Mangus Colorado made no answer. He conferred with his sub-chiefs, and it was agreed to accept money for the death of the brave—the back wages of Jesus Lopez and twenty dollars a month while the Meh-hi-kanos remained at the Copper Mines.

It was not long, however. Their animals began to disappear. They were not brought back. Mimbrenos ceased to go to Santa Rita, ceased to be seen in the hills near by, even in their camps at the Warm Springs. In the next few weeks three hundred head of horses and mules, all fat, and rested and ready for travel, joined the well watched and distant herds of the Apaches. Soldiers went after them but returned empty-handed. In one of these brushes with the soldiers Delgadito in excessive scorn showed himself, and was grazed upon the cheek by a bullet that came twice the distance expected. He did not expose that cheek afterward, nor was he comfortable in the saddle for several days.

Then scouts came flying to the hidden places of the Apaches with word that the Meh-hi-kanos were hurriedly preparing to leave the Copper Mines while there were any horses and mules remaining. It was true, and the Apaches regarded this as a great victory and were inclined to feast over it, as at the end of the great war with the Nakai-yes. But Mangus Colorado was not in the mood for feasting.

The Meh-hi-kanos were many and various, he said. Too much was not to be expected from future parties of Meh-hi-kanos because of the departure of these. It was true Nan-tan Four Eyes departed hastily, while there were a few mules left in his close corrals, but he was nearly ready to depart about further boundary business.

"The work of Nan-tan Four Eyes was with thick-writing, not with war," Mangus Colorado said, "and those soldiers with him were not like other soldiers, but for the protection of the thick-writing only."

Moreover, it was not a time for feasting, said Mangus Colorado, because other Meh-hi-kanos were still rock-scratching in the Mimbreno habitat, and these were very tall and dangerous, different from boundary soldiers, more of the nature of those who died on the Baked Lands. Perhaps these Meh-hi-kanos in the Pinos Altos were of the lost tribe of "Los Go-dammies." In any case they were six men in one, each of these; perhaps seven.

Finally it was not a time for feasting, said Mangus Colorado, since only tontos would take Meh-hi-kanos lightly because the boundary people hurried away. It

might still be a trick. Others might come at any time
with no other orders than to get back three hundred fat
mules and horses and many Apaches also. For the Meh-
hi-kanos were many and various and never to be relied
upon as defeated forever.

LII

E MPTY plaza, silent streets, deserted presidio of Santa
Rital del Cobre, but life was not the same for Mangus
Colorado. The great trap of his mouth closed upon many
things. The more a man thinks through the years, the
more silent he becomes, for his words are not adapted to
those who think little. Cuchillo Negro took life the
same again. He gorged his fill, and slept and gorged
again for many days; then one heard blows in his teepees,
squalling among his women and children, and more and
more braves would come to his fires in the evening, waiting for his raiding challenge. They would talk about
horses, far mountain passes, small villages of the Nakai-
yes—hiding places, water springs. Presently war-dance
would be on, and departure . . . return and feasting again.

That was Cuchillo Negro, that was his father before
him, that was Apache. Such was enough for Coletto
Amarillo, for Ponce, for Delgadito, for Victorio, the silent
and sure. All of these were strong men, discernible in
their separate groups as a single leaf that flutters on a still
bough. All had sons, eye to eye with them by this time,
sons studying the ways of their fathers, preparing to go
the same ways again.

Other young men were coming up; there was Go-khla-
yeh of the narrow head and the thin, wide, twisted
mouth, who had already made three forages into Sonora,
twice returning empty-handed, but the third time with
horses, cattle, prisoners, and spreading abroad the name
the Nakai-yes had given him—Geronimo—an Apache in

the making. That was good. A name is a thing to be made. Mangus Colorado was a name that had been made—

Many had spoken that name—many Nakai-yes, all Mimbrenos; Nan-tan Kan-han-hee had spoken it and left it in his writing for others to see in Was-i-tona, so that all who came this way looked upon the writing first. The Great Father himself had spoken it and Nan-tan Four Eyes, and Iron Belt, and the Medicine Padre before all—the first to put it into Spanish, and at the very last, saying he would come again, but that could not be.

When many men spoke one's name, it was not enough afterward merely for one's own people to speak it. One wanted to hear it again on the tongues of strangers. All Apaches risen among their people wanted to hear the Nakai-yes speak their name, but Mangus Colorado wanted his name to be spoken by the Meh-hi-kanos and also to be written. To be Apache was not enough, when one's name has widely been spoken. Forages and feasting—raids and returns—the smell of dried grass in the teepees, the ninya of a strange people, yet no different—none of these were enough when one has sat at the board with Meh-hi-kanos and felt their greatness even beyond the power of hatred—

That which is finished dies into nothing; only that which is unfinished lives. To deal only with that which is finished is enough for many men; that is Apache. To deal in one's thoughts with that which is unfinished is to be set apart; it is to have thoughts which cannot be spoken to one's own people; it is to move head and shoulders above one's tribe, and hear voices and dream dreams—

Mangus Colorado looked down upon the miners at work in a shallow gorge of the Pinos Altos. They had chosen their main camp at the foot of a long open slope which no one could approach unseen. Many had come— more were coming; their herds were few and closely watched. One could despise the soldiers of the Meh-hi-kanos—all alike, blind to what was before their eyes, and so easily lost, one thought their calling but a trick— yet one could not despise the nan-tans of the Meh-hi-kanos—nor these rock-scratching men with their slow movements and their pipe smoke, and their sitting with rifles across their knees.

They moved slowly; they were never stampeded. They were not thrown into confusion when the boundary people moved out. They were finding gold—not much, but enough to keep them searching for more. Mangus Colorado watched them continually. They filled his eyes through many hours. He told his people that battle not properly prepared for with these miners would cost the Apaches dear. He said a plan was forming in his mind concerning the rock-scratchers, but if much gold were found, his plan would not be possible. Merely an eke of gold continued, however, the miners working half-heartedly.

One day with many Apaches watching behind him, he planted a lance with a white cloth upon it, in sight of the lower camp of the Meh-hi-kanos.

LIII

H E SAW the miners gathering unhurriedly below. Soon a great cloth was waved. As Mangus Colorado stood up from covert and heard the low talk of the warriors about him, his thought was that the walk before him was long, but no ponies had been brought for the silent watching among the rocks.

Also he thought he might have put on the great dress of blue cloth Nan-tan Four Eyes had caused to be made for him, though that had been laughed at once.

It was not a time for haste, and on that walk Mangus Colorado felt himself alone as at no time before in all his days. He was walking out from his own place and his own people. He had not reached his new place and was not at all sure of being welcomed by these people, so that now as he walked he had no place whatsoever, neither old nor new, nor any people.

Moreover, he felt the great weight of his body, the accumulated weight of years. Also the words of the Medicine Padre at the very beginning were clearer in his understanding now than any words since—words not to his liking at the time, words having to do with a bridge.

Now he could see the thick hair they wore on their faces and the stillness of their hands on the rifle stocks. Though he had thought long and carefully about this thing, he now knew that he had been moved to do it by some will greater than his own—

No one stood with outstretched hand. They made no

place for him to sit. They did not appear to watch him closely. He squatted at the edge of their circle. "Tobaho," he said. One tossed him a length of twisted leaf with a bitten end. He closed his teeth upon a portion, and kept the rest. "Cafe," he said.

The Meh-hi-kano nearest stirred and called aloud: "Ramon!" A small one drew near, plainly of the blood of the Nakai-yes. "No cafe aqui," this small one said, explaining that the evening meal was not yet prepared.

"Estamos amigos," said Mangus Colorado.

"Yes, what do you want?"

Ramon, the Nakai-yi who spoke, had an evil look. His chest was very narrow, like the gun that Iron Belt had laughed at because it would shoot only once without reloading.

"I come to speak to the nan-tan of the Meh-hi-kanos," said Mangus Colorado.

Talk and laughter followed, then Ramon said: "Say what you come for. We are listening."

"Chief makes talk with chiefs only—"

When Ramon repeated this, the favorite words of the Meh-hi-kanos were used in their laughter.

"There is no chief among us," said Ramon at length. "Every man for himself. Every man his own chief. This man—" he indicated a red beard with neck very long like a turkey, "this man eats Indians before he feels like smoking in the morning. Fifty to one is his favorite number. He'd talk with you, only you'd have to talk in Commanche or Cheyenne."

"No talk," said Mangus Colorado.

"Pawnee—Arapahoe?"

"No talk. Apache—Navajo all same. Spanish, I myself talk. Chiefs make Spanish talk. Iron Belt say words for Meh-hi-kanos in Spanish. Apache chief comprehend."

"Say it in Spanish—what you come for."

"Apache chief come to see friends. Go away—come again. No make talk to all men. Some day tell Meh-hi-kano nan-tan what he has to say. Make good talk right time—"

He arose. There was silence a moment, then Turkey Neck spoke and Ramon inquired:

"So you've got something to say to the right man?"

"Yes."

"You don't want to say it to all of us?"

"No."

"Well, we all have something to say to you."

"This Indian listens to friend's words."

"What we've got to say is this, big chief: Try any of your tricks on us, try running off any of our stock, for instance, and you and your varmint hide will be so full of cactus prickers it will take your squaws a week to get them out of one side. . . . Sabe hard-rock men? Don't think because Old Lady Bartlett cleared out in a hurry, you can work the same bluff on a lot of hard-rock men. Try and see, Indian."

"Meh-hi-kanos make brave talk," said Mangus Colorado thoughtfully. "Indian much like brave man—Indian go now."

One miner who had not spoken before, slowly got up. His legs were very long. He knocked out his pipe and said a few words to Ramon, who changed his tone:

"If you've got something private to say—this man says he'll listen. This is Dad Evans."

"Big chief Meh-hi-kano?" Mangus Colorado asked.

"Dad's so big, Mister, that Keet Kah-sohn sends for him when he gets in trouble," Roman explained.

Mangus Colorado looked to the north and south and took in the risen Meh-hi-kano in the passing of his glance. He did not find what he sought in the frosty eyes under the faded black hat, although the name of Keet Kah-sohn connected with this miner filled him again with the sense of great need.

"Some day come again. Make talk alone. Indian make plenty talk today. Say adios now."

They permitted him to depart.

LIV

Mangus Colorado did not return to the miner's camp
for two weeks, and this was after extended supervision
of the numbers and activities of the hard-rock men. He
had counted over a hundred and thirty, working along
the gullies and creeks forming the river that flowed into
the sunset without end. They came from settlements on
the Rio Grande and from time to time sent their trains
there with small but heavy packs of ore. These trains
returned with more animals heavily laden, and more men
who began at once chipping the rock and washing the
sands for yellow iron. Their main camp was at the
foot of the long open slope. Each day a portion of the
white men gave themselves to the hunt. Antelope, bear
and wild turkey went down in great numbers before
them and the streams were whipped all day with rods
for the bad-tasting meat from the water.

Mangus Colorado thought over every word of Ramon
(whom he would have been pleased leisurely to take in
his hands and undo) and every look and gesture of the
others. They did not bow the head and make pleasant
talk before talk itself began, as the Nakai-yes did. They
hid their meanings behind laughter, so that no Indian
could understand. Sometimes what they meant to say
came with laughter and sometimes the opposite was intended. Various and confusing were the ways as well
as the kinds of the white men.

On his second visit Mangus Colorado was differently
received. Tobacco was given at once, ready in hand to

smoke, also to eat without swallowing. Though it was the same time of day as before, coffee was put on to boil at his first signal, and was ready when he took his seat on a manta which was spread for him. Turkey Neck was there, also Dad-dad, and this time Ramon was not used to change the talk, but a young yellow-beard with round blue eyes that stayed open like those of a fish. His belt was small as a ninya's, and in loose-hung holsters were pistols with handles of that white stone in which the rainbows are seen. "Hitcha-cock" was the yellow-beard's name. Plainly, though young, he had dealt much with Indians of the north, for he had some words of Navajo and many signs which all Indians understand. Also he had some little Spanish, but of a quality unlike any Mangus Colorado knew. In listening for this, he missed at first much that Hitcha-cock said:

"Glad to see you, Mangus Colorado. How you do? No forget to come again. Good. Last time no ready— bad thing happen—all miners sad and glum—no time make big chief welcome. All better now—"

Mangus Colorado was still going over these words in his mind when Hitcha-cock began again: "Big chief bring word today. Everybody ready listen to Apache talk by this time. Other time big chief no talk—"

In his hands Mangus Colorado had a hot tin-cup of coffee, also tobacco for eating and smoking. "Bad thing happen other time Indian come?" he asked with concern.

"All better now. You—me—go long walk. Make talk alone—What say?"

"White man make much talk before now with sheep Indian in north country?"

"No Navajo—Commanche make talk. Commanche

catch little boy me—stay long time. Squaw say no kill muchacho blue eye me."

It was coming better. Mangus Colorado's mind had been set for Spanish, and had been a trifle slow in adjusting, but now he followed the Indian manner with words and signs. When no more coffee was brought, he consented to walk apart. Still he liked very little the easy gabble of Hitcha-cock or the closed-mouth smiling of those who sat around, with something known to all that waited in their eyes.

"Yellow iron—find plenty?" he asked when they were alone.

"Much sand—little gold. Much rock to break—no big hide-away. No get rich."

"I myself know where plenty gold hides—" said Mangus Colorado. "No good tell many men. Indian talk to one man first."

"Plenty safe tell me," Hitcha-cock laughed. "Big chief plenty gold up his sleeve—huh."

"Sleeve?" Mangus Colorado repeated, wondering how the word of his own name was used.

"No say—Mangus Colorado—" said Hitcha-cock still laughing. "Say Mangus Pesh-klitso—huh."

"Indian no change name—Indian name made for good —all time."

"All right—all right. About this gold—Indian work his own claim?"

"Indian no dig gold. Indian no gold-loco like white man. No good to eat gold—no good smoke. Indian make friend with Meh-hi-kano—long time peace—no break. Much gold here—no. I myself know place where much gold hides. Take white man—go see. White man run to gold—stay where gold is. Indian stay here—keep friends all time."

"Where is all this gold, chief?"

Mangus Colorado pointed casually to the south and east. "Indian and Meh-hi-kano friend take long ride. Go see."

"Take long ride to sand hills?" Hitcha-cock asked with a queer look.

"No sand hills—high mountain place—"

"Apache chief no sabe 'sand hills' in plains Indian talk?"

"No sabe."

"Long ride to sand hills means no come back—"

"Meh-hi-kano friend come back with Indian friend. All Meh-hi-kano men run quick to see gold—when Indian bring friend back to this camp."

"So that's the little idea, chief—"

"Big idea—much gold."

"Too big for me alone, Mangus Colorado. I'll tell you what. Let me tell old Dad Evans about this. Wise hombre—old Dad. Much better let him in—"

"Indian no go to gold cache with many white men one time—"

"Go with two, Mangus Colorado."

"Maybe two—no more. Indian go think now. Come back three days."

"Let me go catch um Dad Evans now. We three make talk—then go apart make thought."

Mangus Colorado at no time trusted Hitcha-cock not to tell the rest or at least part of them. He considered that it might be as well to tell Dad-dad today as another time, yet as he waited his mind was not at peace over what had been done, and in his body was that loss of strength that follows the trickle of many words.

Dad-dad listened carefully, spitting at long intervals, sometimes at a lizard, sometimes at a stone, sometimes at a deer-fly. Only the lizard ever escaped, and not always. It was the thought these Meh-hi-kanos had put upon their rifles, that made them spit straight like that, Mangus Colorado concluded.

One thing had not been considered, said Dad-dad, and that was the matter of the change of boundaries gone into effect since the passing of Old Lady Bartlett—that the Mimbreno country was now in the territory of the Meh-hi-kanos and that the Mother Mountains were in Chihuahua.

"Meh-hi-kanos no 'fraid of Nakai-yes people," said Mangus Colorado.

Hitcha-cock and Dad-dad conferred. No answer was forthcoming to that, but presently the former said:

"Dad thinks the idea very good, Mangus Colorado. He wants some time to think about it. You do also. Just one thing he would like to understand a little better today—"

"Indian make plenty talk today. Come back three days—"

"Just one thing more—why you want us to have gold?"

"Indian no speak in two tongues. Indian want his own land. Want Meh-hi-kano friend, too. Indian no want yellow iron—Meh-hi-kano want yellow iron. Indian show Meh-hi-kano where much yellow iron hides. Meh-hi-kano go there—Indian get his own summer land back—move, stretch himself, sleep, hunt—plenty room. Meh-hi-kano have much gold and say 'Indian friend make me rich. Indian good man—live over there,' he say. Other white men come—leave Indian friend alone—"

Dad-dad pursed his lips, poised his head and let go. The lizard wasn't quick enough that time. "Anyway come back in three days, Mangus Colorado," said Hitchacock at the last.

The thought of Mangus Colorado was to rid his lands of the white miners by showing them the gold creeks Victorio had found in the Mother Mountains, but the thought was not working out to his liking.

LV

Mangus Colorado found them ready for him in his third call. Hitcha-cock took his hand, looked at it, held the palm to the sun. "White-man-friend," he said. "Indian keep word. Come on time. Take long ride today."

"This day—no," said Mangus Colorado. "Another sun make ponies ready. Indian show road to big mountains."

Dad-dad nodded, then led the way down the ravine to the main kitchen; others were there expectantly watching. "Hai, Mangus Colorado," said Ramon, the Nakai-yi. "Welcome, white man's friend."

No smell of coffee in the air, but a great kettle of frijoles was slowly boiling. Turkey Neck moved around from the far side of the fire and held out a hairy freckled hand. Others pressed close. The right hand of Mangus Colorado which Turkey Neck had taken was not released. His left arm was hooked by another. He was rushed. An arm coiled round his neck from behind. Still everyone laughed.

"No do—no like plenty well!" said Mangus Colorado struggling half-heartedly, thinking it was some play like the marked string.

"Indian friend take medicine," said Hitcha-cock. "No get sick on long ride to sand hills."

"No take medicine—Indian chief!" cried Mangus Colorado, but many hands had tightened upon him. He ceased to struggle, to avoid the blackness of a blow upon the head, for Ramon was jumping before his eyes, the

butt of a pistol held ready to strike. "No make trick—
Indian body—old man—much proud."

They laughed loudly at that. His hands were bound,
the rope swung over a white alder limb, his arms pulled
high and taut, the end fastened to the trunk at the base.
Ramon lifted his shirt and tucked the tail into the band
at the neck, baring the back of Mangus Colorado.

"Hai, Apache bull—old bull very strong—" he said,
drawing out the short reserve knife from the breech-
cloth of the prisoner.

"Little bird in the hand for throat of white man friend,"
crooned Hitcha-cock. "Send friend to sand hills when
he sleep—"

Mangus Colorado's eyes fixed on the fire. He saw his
death from that—the long, slow way of the fire. Already
the great review was upon him. Life opening from the
beginning, days standing out—

They were bringing saddle girths, halter shanks, loose
bridle reins from their packs. They gathered about waiting to begin. It was not the fire that they were first intent
upon. Ramon came from the side with a salt-caked
cinch of horse-hair. It was he who knew the least hesitation and prepared the way for others.

"No whip Indian—Apache never forgive!" from Mangus Colorado in a low voice of warning. Again they
laughed, not knowing it was not one man warning another, but race speaking to race.

Ramon's first blow hissed upon him; then others. With
shut eyes he waited; never did the leather fall just as
expected; sometimes before, sometimes afterward. . . .
He was away watching Chawn clizzay. . . . He was
in the teepee with Ko-do. . . . He was crossing his knife

through the bowels of Pindah. . . . He was leading the dun mare, afraid to ride.

"Old bull Indian—pretty proud—never forgive, eh?" called Ramon.

"Strap oil," laughed Hitcha-cock, "leather all sun-dry—very hard. Indian fat make good and soft once more."

He was thinking when they would begin with the fire. . . . He was looking down into the ravine of "Los Go-dammies" . . . down into the cienaga where the Nakai-yes died through the long day . . . ahi-ya-hai! . . . His arrows curved around the long loose back. . . . Old man body finished, but warpath not finished . . . warpath long time forever—

He heard the voices of the white men, but knew not their words, only Ramon drunk and singing with his strokes, and the other voice: "Long ride, Mangus Colorado, long ride to sand hills—pesh klitso mucho. . . . Indian good man, keep his own land—"

His legs wearied; his armpits cracked as the weight of the great body settled. He made no sound. . . . He took his punishment. That was Apache. . . . The strokes were running together into one. The fire would wake him again. . . . "Even so, my brother, we shall meet again."

The strength of his loins ran up his spine to meet the pain; the light of his brain ran down and darkened. . . .

He felt the cold upon his back. His eyes opened to night and firelight. The Meh-hi-kanos were feasting at the fire. There was still light on the western mountains. They had not yet brought the fire. His hands were unbound. He bent forward and placed them on the ground. He gathered his legs under him and felt the earth. He pushed himself up like the son of Placid after lightning struck in the plaza. The white men turned with the fire at their backs. They did not come near or command him down. His feet tramped the turf.

"He's pawing the grass like a pan'ter," Hitcha-cock laughed. "Big chief took his medicine—never say die!"

He started slowly up the ravine. There was no shot behind. They did not call him back.

"Adios—goodnight," sounded the voices. "Send over Apache girls—no whip their backs! Adios, Mangus Colorado—tell that to your lodges. . . . Think out another one, and come back—"

He was moving through the dark, but not toward the Warm Springs or any teepees of his people. He was crossing high country westward. He rested often, slept a little. Daylight found him in Dark Canyons, which he penetrated to his old cache. There he lay in the stream-bed, letting the cold water run over his wounds. He drank and slept and bathed his back and garments. His people were searching for him. When they came near he hid like a wounded beast. No, he would never tell this to the lodges.

On the fourth day he appeared at the Warm Springs, no drop or spatter of blood upon his moccasins, leggings, clout or shirt.

There had been long pow-wow, many words, he said. No end had been reached. The Meh-hi-kanos were not easily to be moved from the summer country of the Mimbrenos. It would come to war, doubtless, but there was no need of haste. Of all his sub-chiefs, Go-khla-yeh, making the name Geronimo, drew nearest, asking the most questions.

LVI

THE BRIDGE had been broken again. He had suffered
the great shame—to be whipped like a dog or a mule.
But shame inflicted in the sight of one's people is one
thing and shame that is borne alone another. At no
time was his bare back uncovered to the sun, nor did he
sit with others as aforetime in the steam of the Warm
Springs. He lay down to sleep in none of his teepees,
lest he cry out the secret in his sleep. He kept his
thoughts still when others drew near.

Had his people been present, though every blow were
felt to the quick by the tribe, his power would have been
broken among them. A body that Usen permitted to be
violated at the hands of the enemy would have become
unsanctified as that of an adulterous squaw. Only one
thing would have restored him in the sight of his people—
instant sweeping retribution. Mangus Colorado was not
prepared for that. He did not care for fury-fighting; it
was not his way to leap to the warpath and promulgate
his strategies on the run.

Yet solemn and terrible were his thoughts. One by one
he went over the incidents of his first, second and third
visits to the miners' camp. Also he went over the blows
to the time counting was lost, when the taste of death
was in his mouth, the sight of his own death a vision before his eyes.

Life was simple again; the vague vast gropings of his
thoughts toward the long-time peace, toward an allegiance with Meh-hi-kanos and their inevitable increase, yet

keeping intact the habitat of his people—all this went out in the whipping. He had become Apache again—the Enemy—but an Apache with a brain. He had been mortally wounded. He had seen his end—the fighting death. He would not go down in the thick-writing of the Meh-hi-kanos as a friend, but as "an arm raised above many tribes, an arm red with blood to the elbow." The fighting death was the thing. The Medicine Padre had seen far that day.

Compared to this, the death of Soldado Fiero was a little and meagre death, and the death of Cuchillo Negro, his son. For while the wounds of Mangus Colorado still ached and scalded under his hunting shirt, a runner came over the Divide from Sonora with the word of Cuchillo Negro's end at the hands of a Nakai-yi woman, a prisoner of the day. She had taken his own knife as he lay. She had opened his body and her own, before they found her in the dark of the shelter of boughs. Cuchillo Negro had called but once.

The messenger was gray from his night-and-day running. Another Mexican prisoner had escaped in the excitement. The Sonora soldiers would be emboldened and would gather doubtless in great numbers, to get back their herds and prisoners.

Apart Mangus Colorado mourned the one who was never his friend, but Apache always. He permitted Go-khla-yeh to go with thirty men, and Delgadito with fifty to follow more slowly and help bring in the herds. To Shi-ka-she he sent word that his presence would be an honor at this time. The Chihuicahui chieftain came at once.

"It is not that the warriors of the Chihuicahuis will be

needed, but the counsel of my friend is greatly desired," said Mangus Colorado.

Together they spent days scouting along the ridges above the miners; studying their position in relation to every open slope and canyon curve. Their main camp at the foot of a long open grade almost treeless, was a confusion to the Apache idea of attack. At the top was a heavily-wooded bench admirable for ambush, but no way appeared to draw the miners there. Sometimes Victorio, now second in command of the entire Mimbreno people, accompanied them but more often they were alone. Mangus Colorado spoke of that short gun with the fat chest using six shots without pause. Shi-ka-she brought word even more terrifying—of a many-shots gun of full-length, with the firestone fastened to the ball itself, and capable of carrying so far that a man looked no bigger than a gopher on a mound.

This was grave news. Mangus Colorado said he was aware of the great distance possible from the creasing of Delgadito, but not of the many loads contained. He did not believe that the miners under consideration had any such death-dealing guns. Still one never knew what the next pack-train might bring from the Meh-hi-kano settlements on the Rio Grande. He suggested that someone very high in the medicine lodge at Was-i-tona must be sitting to no other purpose than changing the rifles of the Meh-hi-kanos for the better.

"All that they do is for yellow iron," said Shi-ka-she.

"Yet they must find it for themselves or they do not believe," said Mangus Colorado.

If Shi-ka-she rightly heard that, he could not know how the knowledge was bought. But Shi-ka-she at that moment was thinking of his friend who had not failed.

"In the words of Keet Kah-sohn of the Meh-hi-kanos, one rock-scratcher with two small mules is more to be feared by our people than many soldiers," said Shi-ka-she. "For it is he who finds first what all white men seek."

The Chihuicahui then told of doings far to the north and westward—of the finding of gold in the last of rivers beyond the backbone of the world, of a string of wagons stretching from Was-i-tona to the very end of the land where the sun goes down, of great tribes of whites gathered there thick as bees in their hive-changing times, of their fighting together and toiling over a single river, not pausing to bury their dead—

It was for words like this that Mangus Colorado had called his friend to counsel. For of all Apaches, Shi-ka-she alone shared his restless fascination for the Meh-hi-kanos, and alone could look out of things finished into that which lay in store to be accomplished.

". . . through the lands of the Kiowas, their wagons stretched, through the lands of the Commanches, the Pawnees, the Cheyennes leaving them desolate . . . scattering the cimmaron," continued Shi-ka-she . . . "Let us look to the Sun, brother, and pray to Usen that yellow iron may not be hiding in these mountains in abundance to bring the white torrent upon us, nor in the mountains of my people—"

The two chiefs scattered hoddentin to the sun as its rim was cut by the peaks of the Chihuicahuis. They sat in silence together, then Shi-ka-she departed, leaving Mangus Colorado to begin his new war.

LVII

A STRANGE thing was seen toward the top of the long slope above the miners' camp where Mangus Colorado had planted his lance of truce. Apache ninyas and young squaws congregating there in the late afternoon to remain until dark. They were not seen to look down; they made no sign to the Meh-hi-kanos. Their voices were not raised, but they were plainly observed to be braiding their hair at sunset-time.

Meanwhile, teepees vanished from the Warm Springs and the old ridge above Santa Rita. All Mimbrenos were on the move, hiding by day in Dark Canyons or far to the westward to the grass slopes. All fighting men and boy-men were deeply instructed in particular caution and the instant readiness for flight. The herds were kept in close watch, with orders for them to be driven across toward the Baked Lands in case of alarm. The warriors were encouraged to familiarize themselves with their guns, for all important men were fire-armed by this time, in addition to their bows and knives, but it was never possible to train Apaches to shoot at nothing. Powder and ball was too valuable to waste in target practice. Next to horses these things were beyond price for gambling, with the proviso that all such goods were to be re-distributed at the call to the warpath.

All this time the lithest of young women played among the rocks, showing themselves even at noon when the miners came down the gullies to the fires, and dressing their hair or braiding one another's at close of day. To

the voices shouted up at them, they made no answer, and
when the miners started toward them in the dusk, they
took flight like birds.

One day a pack-train that had left camp for the Rio
Grande settlements was attacked on a narrow ledge trail
within three hours after setting out. The firing was
from covert across the canyon. The mules were stampeded, several going overside, the miners flattened against
the cliff, or picked off as they ran forward or back. Not
an Apache was seen; the fallen were not approached, the
firing quickly over. At the same time three small bands
of white hunters abroad in the mountains were ambushed
and destroyed. All this before midday, and again, as if
nothing had happened, Apache ninyas showed themselves in the bright sun among the rocks.

All was silence below; the white men moving quickly
about with no sound. The full company foregathered,
standing together in small changing groups, their voices
not heard, pouring their coffee as they stood.

Then at a certain moment twenty-five whites quickly
broke out from the separate knots and started up the
slope. This time the Indian girls departed tardily, as if
loathe to leave—making smothered sounds of excitement
and broken laughter. They kept together in their flight
toward the timber. The miners came after them, not
running, but grim-faced, no look of play or dalliance
now. They entered the shadow of the trees, penetrating
the thickly wooded bench. A few broke into a run—

One shot—then a hundred—then scattered shots and
arrows into the bodies of those fallen but still fighting;
a swift re-arranging of the ambush for those now running up from camp—

Silence had fallen again; the few who escaped carried word of the overwhelming Apache party in the upper woods, and the Meh-hi-kanos no longer risked leaving camp. Among the fallen bodies, Mangus Colorado had paused over one, a yellow-beard. It was warm but motionless. He bent to lift a sagging eyelid, no recognition there, but more than ever fish-like in its glassy stare. He took the two pistols with handles of rainbow stone and left the body to the squaws.

Such was his first day's work—there could be no other like this—forty men, one third of the entire company of Meh-hi-kanos, had been counted on the ground. One for each blow possibly, though he could not tell precisely the number that had fallen upon him. Toward sundown he sent back the ninyas to braid their hair among the rocks.

LVIII

O NE DAY before the late summer rains, Mangus Colorado burned the grass along the main slope, and all the forage patches adjacent to the ravines where the miners worked. Later he concentrated on a sizable pack-train headed for the diggings. Another of his coups was the fouling of their water supply with dead animals. He was without haste; he had nothing else to do. He kept his own Apaches gaunt from sustained stealth; but he also crazed the enemy with incessant strain. When they dashed out for reprisal they found nothing but virgin forests, primeval silence, and a despoiled camp upon their return. Mangus Colorado counted no expenditure of labor or time too great for one clean shot. All tendencies to feasting were checked by the sentence:

"The Meh-hi-kanos are still in our mountains—"

To the Apache mind the ruse of the ninyas was an inimitable morsel. It bordered on the supernatural. Their venerable chieftain was seen in a shine of unparalleled prowess. They weighed his long delaying, the leisureliness of his several goings to the miners' camps, his exactly timed and exactly calculated strokes. That which is done must be sung, but these things were sung in snatches.

Apaches were flighty, he burned with a steady flame. They lived in the present and called it good, to him the present contained a measure of past and future. Where their thoughts ended, his began; triumphs that satisfied them merely kept alive his insatiable zeal. To them the

242

Meh-hi-kanos were but mortals after all, more deadly than the Nakai-yes, but helpless in extremity; to him they were insuperable, regardless of the present plight of the hungry and harried few in the Pinos Altos ravines. When the miners finally left the Pinos Altos, the Mimbrenos regarded this as the consummation of their warmaking, but Mangus Colorado said, "They will come again."

In this he was most dangerous, that at the moment of victory he was more cautious than ever; that the first law of his code was never to underestimate the adversary.

At the end of his great three-tined campaign against the Nakai-yes after the plaza massacre, there had come a day in which law was restored, war ended and feasting begun. There was no such day for the Mimbrenos again. War with the Meh-hi-kanos never ended. Cuchillo Negro and his father before him had lived the double life of raiding and resting, but Mangus Colorado never rested, and never was the promise of intense activity so sure as at the end of his long silent thinkings. Even the children were hushed when he sat alone. Never again would it be said that long peace had made the Apaches unwary. The eyes and fingers of Mangus Colorado were constantly at work on every border. Scouts were taught that no sound was more ominous than the tap of iron hammers on the rock; a solitary stranger with more thought of his tools than his fire-arms set the Mimbreno nation on the jump—

Yet one of these was allowed to enter, for the queer reason that his actions were those of one whose mind has lost its way. The long hair of this one was very thin and white. He wore no hat. He stood long and silently in the high places, his empty hands raised over the valleys. He would walk a little way, then stand and turn around. Such an one it was profanation to kill. His packs were very thin; his thoughts turned rarely to food, though his burros were fat with slow travel and easy feeding by the way. Scouts came to Mangus Colorado saying:

"We did not shoot, because of his mind-gone-far appearance."

Mangus Colorado went to see and the white-haired ancient made him think of the Medicine Padre's last coming to the ridge. They took him in, but his language was uninterpretable. He lingered through a winter by the Mimbreno fires. The dogs forgot their hatred of the stranger; the children played about him unmindful of his presence. Mangus Colorado often sat across the fire in contemplation, but the stranger talked with his gods and not with men. In spring he arose as one rested and looked for his burros and tools, but when he was restrained from going, he sat down again peaceably enough. His gaze went out upon the mountain-tops until one day a child brushing against him toppled him sideways and he was gone. This was Mangus Colorado's only white guest.

LIX

THEN CAME bitter medicine. Shi-ka-she had taken the white man's road. The man-travel wagons of the whites were crossing his lands unmolested. He permitted them to raise roofed shelters and corrals at the very foot of his stronghold. He entered into a covenant with them to supply wood for their fires and cut grama grass for their horses. He protected them from Coyoteros and outlaw bands of Nakai-yes and mixed bloods.

Shi-ka-she had permitted his name to go forth among them as a friend, and this name on the white man's tongue became Chies, then Co-chies (Cochise). Shi-ka-she had become the bridge.

The sun was going down on the long day of Mangus Colorado. The sun was still high, but it had been higher. It was nearer the night than the morning side. He had cleared his borders of the enemy only to find himself cooped inside. The Mimbrenos were happy because their thoughts did not go out over their borders; but the thoughts of Mangus Colorado had moved out over unfinished worlds and were now forced back. He had fulfilled the highest measure of the Apache, but it was not enough.

Shi-ka-she said, "Come."

In his word was allegiance; the opening of the land of the Mimbrenos together with the land of the Chihui-cahuis; acceptance of the Mimbreno by the Meh-hi-kanos on the same terms as Shi-ka-she's people.

"Come, it is not too late," said Shi-ka-she, but this

word could not be accepted by the older from the younger
chieftain. It had been in the thought of Mangus Colorado to speak this word to Shi-ka-she—to Kutu-hala, to
Co-si-to, and then to the Great Nan-tan of all nan-tans
of the Meh-hi-kanos to say: "These are my younger
brothers. They are with me and I am with you—" in
the making of the long peace. Such a word could not
come from one who had stumbled upon it without sufficient pondering. And Shi-ka-she had not fallen under
the lash; his blood had not softened the leathers of the
laughing Meh-hi-kanos. . . .

Mangus Colorado raised his eyes to the sun, but its
flash was not the same blinding shield of his youth; he
sat thinking in the steam of the hot springs, but his
thoughts came back to him rejected from over the borders. He sat among things that were finished, and his
strength abated within him. Only when his borders were
threatened, he arose and became the scourge, his eyes
canny with prowess long proven. It was then that his
people knew him again, but in their own stiff-necked
way they loved him always.

At last came a message from Shi-ka-she, and this time
the word did not say, "Come," but "I am coming!"

LX

THE WHITE men are truce-killers," said Shi-ka-she.

It was seen that his knee was stiffened with a wound, as he stepped down from his horse. Mangus Colorado had met him at the end of the hills bordering the grass. They did not go eastward to the Warm Springs, but climbed the ridge above the Santa Rita del Cobre for immediate counsel.

"Peace has ended between the Chihuicahuis and the Meh-hi-kanos. My brother will listen—"

Mangus Colorado bowed.

They were seated alone. Smoke was blown. Shi-ka-she placed his hands together and regulated his breath as if many words pressed upon him. He did not look at Mangus Colorado but into the west from whence he had come. He told of his work with the whites, saying that he had kept his word to the letter supplying wood and dried grass; that no evil had overtaken white travelers in his country, but that four days ago a party of white soldiers from the fort appeared in the foothills of his stronghold and raised the white flag for talk.

Shi-ka-she with two of his brothers, the brother of one of his wives and three younger men of his household, hurried down at once and stood before the bluecoats of whom there were thirteen—twelve common soldiers and a boy-man* at the head, this being a way frequently of the Meh-hi-kanos to put grown men with beards under

---

*Lieut. Geo. N. Bascom, U. S. Army.

the leadership of one fresh from herd-watching, squaw milk not yet dried out of his blood.

"Face to face we stood, and this I saw," said Shi-ka-she, "that there was not in his head that with which to make his eyes fair-dealing. Though his fathers had given him distinction, he was of the tontos among the whites who do not see one Indian as differing from another, nor the war lord of a people as one carrying authority. Yet I had nothing to fear, my covenant with his people being fulfilled. He was without signs and means of talk, except bravado, but one of his men made talk in Spanish for him; and this man demanded of me cattle that had been stolen from a rancher on the Sonoita river, also the return of a boy of seven years taken at the same time. I knew nothing of these things, but said I would see what I could find out about them for the soldiers and report on the following day."

The next day the same two parties met at the same place, the white soldiers having made camp at the station of the man-travel wagons, and pitched a large white shelter there in the shape of an Indian teepee (Sibley tent). Shi-ka-she said he had nothing to report so far; that he had sent out runners to learn what they could, but they had not returned. He believed that the trouble was caused by a band of Coyoteros* known to have been in the country recently, but more time would be required to make sure of this. Then to their astonishment Shi-ka-she and his friends were arrested and taken to the great white tent.

---

*This was later proved true. The affair happened to be probed by authorities, because of the sudden widespread interest in the kidnapping. The boy was Mickey Free, whose name became a "household word" throughout the States.

Mangus Colorado noted Shi-ka-she's anger, but deeper than anger a strange grief in the heart of his friend.

"There was at this time in charge of the man-travel station for the Meh-hi-kanos, one white man we called Beela-chezzi (Crooked Fingers), who all the time made practice in Apache talk and paid money to my people fresh, and fresh for sticks and dried grass. Many times when I myself come to the station Beela-chezzi say to me, 'Cochise, I am Indian friend,' and now when I am in the big tent with my kinsmen, and very angry, Beela-chezzi come to me and say with his breath, 'Cochise, my friend, I am grieved! This fool Teniente Shave-tail does not know any better. He does not know big Indian chief from common buck. I am against him, also his soldiers are against him, but he is in command until other soldiers come from the fort. All will then come right, my friend. Trust me. Teniente's back will be strictly peeled from this—"

Shi-ka-she explained that his blood was running black with anger at this time. Apache-wise he had turned his back upon Beela-chezzi and walked among his friends in the white light of the big cloth, the soldiers pacing outside. Dark was coming. Then Shi-ka-she whispered that he meant to escape, but advised the six others to wait until he could return with warriors. From his breech-cloth he drew out a small reserve knife and when it was full dark, slit the canvas on the side from which came fewest sounds. His friends said they preferred to follow him than to wait, but the alarm sounded outside the instant Shi-ka-she was clear. Soldiers ran for him with long knives on their rifles, but he leaped through them, escaping with a deep cut above the knee. The others were re-captured.

That night Shi-ka-she gathered his warriors and drove off the station horses and made prisoners of two white men coming from the Sonoita. At daybreak, they took position near the station, just out of gunshot. Beela-chezzi was seen coming toward them, and was permitted to approach for talk. He said that Tonto Teniente was full of wrath over the stolen horses and meant to take it out on the six friends of Shi-ka-she if the horses were not returned at once. Shi-ka-she pointed to his two prisoners and said that they would be exchanged for his people, and the horses sent back with them. Beela-chezzi said there was no dealing with the young officer, that the lives of Cochise' friends were in danger, but if Cochise would accede for the present to unfair demands, all would be made straight when more soldiers came from the fort under a nan-tan who would put the shave-tail under arrest at once.

Shi-ka-she breathed evenly several times before speaking again to Mangus Colorado:

"Because of that which was already done, I could not see Beela-chezzi for my friend. 'Send me back my people and I will send the horses and my prisoners,' I made answer, but Beela-chezzi shook his head again, saying, 'That would be fair among men, Cochise, but we are dealing with a madman. For the sake of your people, do this. All will be known in two days more. I give you my word.' Again I said to Beela-chezzi, 'Go with my decision—' but at that moment one of my white prisoners taken in the night broke away and ran toward the man-travel station. My people sent shots after him, but he was not brought down until close to the Meh-hi-kanos and it was not the rifles of my warriors, but theirs that killed him, their eyes blinded with fear believing we had begun an attack. Then Beela-chezzi said, 'They have one and all eaten the Teniente's loco-weed!' With that he started for the station, but my people stopped him—"

Shi-ka-she paused and turned to Mangus Colorado.

"I myself did not say no to that," he added. "Then shouting began from the white soldiers. I commanded silence from my people for Beela-chezzi to listen and interpret. As he listened his face was of one who looks on death. Also the white prisoner who remained with us heard his own death in the shouts of the Meh-hi-kanos and made answer at the top of his voice, 'No! No! No!' Beela-chezzi said, 'The madman means to hang your six friends, if the horses are not returned at once.' 'He will not dare to do that,' I said. 'Yes, Cochise, he thinks it is his duty to teach the Apache a lesson. Accede to his demands—no one has a chance, if you fail us.' I could not believe and told him to answer that we would kill our prisoners and many others. 'Would you kill me, Cochise?' 'Tell him so,' I said. This he shouted to them and the answer of the Meh-hi-kanos was the stringing up of my brother, the others also being made ready.

"We took the garments from our prisoner, and held up his body for them to see and hear his cries. Then it was that Beela-chezzi broke and ran. One of my warriors spurred his horse after him, caught him with a reata and veered back toward us, dragging the body at full gallop. I had not intended to do that, but the thing was done. Our own people were hanging by the neck, their feet unbound. Such was the day."

Both chiefs were silent a moment before Shi-ka-she resumed:

"I come to unite with the wise one of all our people, if so he will accept one who has trusted his heart in the hands of strange men—"

The older man bowed.

"I come," added Shi-ka-she, "to unite the Chihuicahuis with the Mimbrenos in war against the truce-killers, until one hundred have fallen for each one of my household that was hanged. I have fully spoken."

Mangus Colorado's immediate answer was not in words. He sat motionless a moment and then began slipping his shirt over his head from behind. He turned to Shi-ka-she whose eyes fixed upon the scarred ridges and ruffled welts—

"They are a mixed people. What one does, another undoes," said Mangus Colorado. "While we have friends among them, the many are without understanding. It is not our part to cleave to them. Until this time, my brother, no one has looked upon these wounds, but for each stroke many white men already have fallen. This too, was done under the white flag for truce."

LXI

THUS BEGAN the deadly combination of Mangus Colorado and Cochise. From the land of the Kiowas on the east to the land of the Papagos and Opatas in the west, they combed and screened the country of rock-scratchers, traders, trappers, ranchers and soldiers. Yet the Meh-hi-kanos came unceasingly as the river that flows unto the sunset, and increasingly as that river widens into unknown lands. The vow of Cochise was fulfilled, and for the disbelief of one white officer that the Coyoteros took the cattle from the Sonoita rancher, Americans were raided of horses and mules that would stretch from the Rio Grande to the sea.

Still the white men came with their traps and their tools, with bigger wagons and ever more deadly guns. Higher and higher was the price which the Apache paid as the score piled up.

There was one day that fixed itself in Apache tradition above all others—the Day of the Six Tall Men.*

Signal smokes had bellied up from the peak at the east end of Big Medicine Pass in the Chihuicahuis. Six men with long beards and fringed coats—with saddle and pack animals riding easily to the west—were already in the throat of the canyon, shadows closing upon them. Apaches fired; they did not stampede. They did not even dismount. They looked forward, backward. One chose to keep going, so they pushed ahead. The Apaches followed along the canyon walls. Several hundred had

*The "Free" Thompson party of frontiersmen, 1860.

253

rallied at the signal—the two great war lords working together in the country of Cochise.

One of the whites huddled forward on his mule; another held him in the saddle, until the canyon widened. They looked forward toward water but could not reach it without coming into close range again. They dismounted, and unhurriedly began to tie the legs of their animals. From the packs they set down boxes, rolled together a breastwork of rocks. They sat on the ground, lit their pipes, then dropped lower looking for something to shoot at.

Whenever one pulled a trigger, there appeared to be a reason for it. This Mangus Colorado early noticed, but the extreme rarity of their shots led him to believe they were short on ammunition. He agreed with Cochise to risk a charge. The Apaches closed in. The firing that they met was not excessive, but the Apaches perceived themselves frightfully thinned. They were driven back with twenty dead, others badly wounded, and so astonished that their fallen were not picked up until darkness.

Apart from the unprecedented shock of loss, there were two peculiarities about that charge; there were more dead than wounded; and those wounded were by no means grazed. Then from their coverts, they saw the whites passing a canteen and lighting their pipes again. One rose to his knees to cut the throat of a mule that was "running on its side," as the Apaches say of a grass-eating animal in its death throes.

Another charge was made next daybreak with a bad loss. Throughout that day the Apaches drew back farther and farther from the inspired eyes of that dwindled company, but still an occasional shot found its mark, and those who had been wounded died with a certainty that gave pause, if not palsy, to those alive.

At least three of the whites had been still so long there could be no mistake, but the Apaches had paid ten to one for them. No result was worth that. The end was waiting; waterless waiting for the whites, with the sound of the water in their ears. It was not that day, nor the next, that the last man, uncoupled from a bullet, hunched himself forward on his elbows up the canyon toward that haunting sound. The Apaches were a bit awed by that last man: they let him drink, partly—

His right arm from shoulder to elbow was jet-black from the kicking recoil of his gun through three full days. Even now his ammunition was unspent. The Apaches put no mark upon his body, but thirst had blackened his mouth. The protruding tongue made no secret of torture of two full days.

"The Meh-hi-kanos are brave men," said Cochise.

"The Meh-hi-kanos are of many kinds," said Mangus Colorado, "and some are very brave."

LXII

Aʟʟ ᴛʜᴀᴛ had been was as nothing to what now appeared. The Meh-hi-kanos were at war. It was not the Nakai-yes this time, but war among themselves. Those in gray coats who came from the land east of the Mescaleros were at war with blue coats who came from the north, also with those who came from the west. All Apache places were broken by their invasions; the land drummed with the tramp of many feet.

There was no rest. Warpath, which once brought life and freshness to Indian days and made times of feasting and the singing of deeds possible, had already been sustained until the tribes were crazed with exertion. The blood of one's enemy on the ground held no joy, for the blood of one's friends mingled with it.

All wild game was driven to remote places. There had been no time for replenishing raids; horse stock was low for food and travel; the hooves of war-ponies worn to the quick, their paunches lumpy with sticks and weeds to keep from starving. Women and children ran wild in the canyons, hunted hither and thither, no teepee life possible.

The hands of Mangus Colorado trembled; the taste had gone out of his meat. He longed for the Warm Springs to sweat the weariness from his bones, longed for deep draughts of tuh-le-pah and maguay roasts to bring back the oil to his blood. Beyond all this was his longing for the return of silence that he might find the laws of his life again. He had balanced his score with the enemy, but the enemy had no sense of it. The Meh-hi-kanos came for more, continually, counting their losses and sufferings as nothing if they could but gain their mysterious ends of war with one another. The very meaning of law was gone from the world.

While fighting in the unpleasant country of Shi-ka-she, word reached Mangus Colorado that Meh-hi-kanos were in the Pinos Altos. He separated his Mimbrenos from the Chihuicahuis and returned to his country. What he found was men neither of the blue nor the gray, but rock-scratchers at the old diggings again. Moreover, they were in such numbers that he would require the help of Shi-ka-she to rout them out.

Message of this was sent therefore to his younger brother. Runners brought back word from Shi-ka-she that Meh-hi-kanos in quantities such as never before had been seen were coming from the west and straight toward his stronghold. If Mangus Colorado would come again and help him, Shi-ka-she said he would return with his Chihuicahuis and help retake the mountains of the Mimbrenos.

There was no rest. He rallied his warriors and once more crossed the grass. It was even as Shi-ka-she said. From mountain-range to mountain-range—greater than the war party of Nan-tan Kah-han-hee—the new column of white men* was coming from the west, its point aimed at the Chihuicahuis, even at the Big Medicine Pass where the Six Tall Men had been finished before reaching the springs.

"In all these mountains, there will be no place for my people if the Meh-hi-kanos come this way," mourned

---

*Gen. Carleton's California volunteers eastward-bound for Civil War service.

Shi-ka-she, "yet already their scouts are camped one sun from here at the Whan-see-kee springs.* Between their camp at this time and Medicine Pass there is no water but there is water to the northward. If they can be kept from entering here, they will be forced northward around the mountains, and my stronghold will not be invaded—"

That night the scouts of the Meh-hi-kanos were on the march again straight toward Big Medicine Pass. The combined warriors of Mangus Colorado and Shi-ka-she lined the canyon where the Pass narrowed; nearly five hundred Apaches, yet when they remembered what Six Tall Men had done on this same battleground, the Meh-hi-kanos advance guard of ten horsemen and thirty foot soldiers now approaching were not to be taken lightly.

For hours Mangus Colorado watched from his signal peak. At times his heart burned with the old fire, and the weariness dropped from him. Shi-ka-she drew near and watched in silence by his side. They had made their covenant together that these whites should not reach Big Medicine water—a word rarely taken by Apache chiefs for it involved possible losses in warriors unthinkable to ordinary strategy. But this was Shi-ka-she's home resort, Big Medicine Springs his central treasure. If the vanguard of the Meh-hi-kanos was flung back athirst the whole army might be turned north around the mountains. This would send the Meh-hi-kanos into the Mogollons on their eastern course, instead of into the Pinos Altos. Thus Mangus Colorado would be benefitted also.

"Two small wagons are with them," said Shi-ka-she.

*Dragoon Springs, Arizona, forty miles from water in the Chihuicahuis, now the Chiricahuas. Big Medicine is now called Apache Pass.

"It is water they are carrying in casks covered with cloth—"

Mangus Colorado looked again and his knees weakened. For matters close at hand, his eyes blurred often, but for distance the years had not impaired them. "Not wagons for water, my brother, but fire-wagons—a hundred rifle tubes in one."

"We will watch when they make them ready and give them nothing to fire at—" said Shi-ka-she.

There was no rest.

In the late shadows of afternoon, the Meh-hi-kanos filed into the Pass. The animals smelled the water and hurried forward. Mouths of men were open from the long dusty march. They saw nothing, thought of nothing, but drink. For hours their only fear was that men had lied about water ahead. Now they knew it was no lie, for the animals had come to life. A single—pn-n-ng—then a crash of rifles from both sides of the gorge—shots pouring down upon the narrow file of white men strung along the trail.

The Meh-hi-kanos bent forward as if passing through a storm. Animals were down; the voice of the nan-tan was raised, and one by him with the brass throat repeated his orders above the scream of horses. The soldiers on their knees or flat among the rocks had only the smoke-puffs to fire at. Their shots flattened upon the rocks. The Apaches took good care of that.

Horses with empty saddles and mules with the packs found themselves loose and climbed the trail toward the springs.

Minutes lengthened, shadows deepened. The Meh-hi-kanos were taking severe punishment without giving any in return. At no time were the covers taken from the fire-wagons. Retreat was bad enough, but to fall back from water which was life itself—

Yet night was falling. There was no other way. The trumpeter sounded a strange call. The Apaches answered with exultant whoops for the Meh-hi-kanos were turning back.

Beating their animals, they kept their diminished line, carrying or supporting their wounded, making no pretense to answer the fire which the Apaches still concentrated upon them. Into the open foothills where there was still daylight though the sun had set, they bowed under a fire from either flank.

Mangus Colorado directed the good-measure attack from the south side—Cochise from the north. The last horseman of the Meh-hi-kanos was cut off by Apaches on Shi-ka-she's side. He spurred in the opposite direction and was making a big circle through Mangus Colorado's warriors when a bullet dropped his horse.

He stepped clear in the fall, lifted his carbine from its boot, dropped behind his kicking horse and leisurely chose his mark. Mangus Colorado pulled up his horse's head for a screen as the carbine spurted. He did not hear the crack of that carbine, but a strange squaw-like murmuring from his own men. He was in the midst of it. His horse was taken from him. Night had thickly settled. He was in the thick of many warriors—many voices, many pressing hands.

LXIII

A soft falling rain. Blood of his body was running out
of its natural course. He could not now rightly breathe;
one side was choked with wet heat. . . . No rest from
many wars, yet on his last day the Meh-hi-kanos were
driven back. They would remember. Nan-tan Kah-han-
hee had remembered. It was written—

The rain was falling harder. They covered his face.
He had covered the faces of men—faces of men too brave
for the knife or the fire. Covered and left them—

Gusts of wind tore the cover from his face. Sheets of
water, lightning flashes in which he saw the bare bodies
—sometimes four, sometimes six—of those who carried
him. He heard their gasping under his great weight.

Thus Soldado Fiero had been carried up and over the
great Divide. All were gone—Soldado Fiero—Cuchillo
Negro, his son—Delgadito—Ponce—Coletto Amarillo—
Wano-boono—Aña . . . an old old man in the rain—

He knew the voices of those running near—Victorio
and another, Geronimo. Victorio of few words was not
gone. Geronimo of many words was not gone.

The litter-bearers were changing. They were running
easily now. He could sink again. There was an inner
silent place of ease where his breath was not choked,
where the wind did not roar and the rain did not reach—
where the teepee flaps did not fight the storm nor the
branches whip against it. There was no heat, nor any
cold, nor light of day, yet it was not dark there.

A deluge of water angered him. No, they had not

thrown water upon his face. It was the storm. They were not keeping him awake with torture. It was the wind and the rain. . . . He had been shot—the battle over, all but one man—then his own time had come. His people were running with him—hours upon hours—through a night that had no end. Always as he sank into that place of ease, a torrent of water struck his face. Sometimes the change of litter-bearers brought him back.

He was cold. It was the crawling cold of old-man limbs. He knew the great heat. He called for breath, the blinding day was in his eyes. . . . Jornado del Muerto. . . . They were running with him to the Womb of the Mother—many were hurrying with him—all Mimbreno warriors had stopped the war because he had stopped. At last in the great heat, he found his voice, "Victorio!"

The strong and silent one bent close as he ran.

"Where—why?"

"Janos—soon!"

War with the Nakai-yes. . . . There was no rest. . . . His throat closed upon words. He sank into the ease, but voices brought him back—Geronimo speaking in the language of the Nakai-yes:

"Many Indian come—no come for war. Big chief very low. Many Indian bring big chief for Janos medicine man to make well. No come to fight—no kill."

The village had closed upon them. Cries of women from the houses. The medicine man was found and led forward. . . .

"Make big chief well again—many Indian go 'way—no fight. Big chief die—medicine man die, too—many people die!"

Such were the terms of ministration—such the fee of

life or death for him whose shaking hands worked at the burning core of the pain, whose wires turned and searched in the shattered place. He made no cry. That was Apache. A voice was calling!

He was in the still place. There were stars, yet the light was more than starlight. The winds blew cool and one was coming toward him—the white uncovered head. They stood together on the high clear ridge.

". . . even as I promised, my brother. Long have I tarried for this meeting while you were moiling in the dust. All struggle, all clashing together is but mystification of the dust. As I saw but darkly—so you have seen but darkly, but nothing is yet finished—nothing lost. That which we began together will be taken up with more light. A little longer in the dust—be of good courage, and you will understand—"

LXIV

THERE was rest. In the desert when they laid him down; rest also in the stronghold of the Chihuicahuis. Nothing was asked of him; he had no lands to protect, no wars to make, no thinking for other men, no words to say. All his life he had never stopped until now. All his thinking, all his deeds—had amounted to something other than he supposed, but it did not greatly matter. He did not mystify others by trying to tell what he now considered.

Of all that had happened save one thing, this alone was most meaningful: that his warriors to the last man had forgotten the enemy when he fell; that they had run with him through a whole night of storm and much of the next day; that they entered the presidio itself and forced the enemy to minister to his needs.

As Victorio said: "Our people knew no fear of the soldiers at Janos; they were carried forward by the sudden great need. When their war-lord bowed forward in the saddle, they did not even pause to kill the white soldier."*

The battle with the Meh-hi-kanos was finished for one day only. The Meh-hi-kanos had returned to the Pass the next day with more men and wagons and Iron Belt himself, darkly remembered of the company of Nan-tan Four

---

*Trooper John Teal, of Captain Cremony's command in the California Column. His story is extraordinary. After firing his shot at one he knew to be an Apache chief, he suddenly found himself alone, all the Indians vanishing in the dark. It was not enough for him to escape with his life, but he loosed the cinch of his dead horse and carried the saddle eight miles to rejoin his command.

Eyes. The Chihuicahuis had not known him, but the wounded of the Mimbrenos who could not help carry their wounded chief to Janos, had known him and liked not his coming. In the second day's battle, the Chihuicahuis alone met the enemy, and the Meh-hi-kanos had not entered the Pass single-file as before. They spread out along the canyon sides driving all before them. Halted by the stern fire of the Apaches from the springs, they paused only to bring up their fire-wagons. The Chihuicahuis not having felt the deadliness of these, continued to hold their shelters behind the rocks and trees at the springs until the canyon roared with the great noise. Many were dead, many could not rise; those who could, left for the high places among the peaks, forgetting all else, even the bodies of their companions.

"One who has not seen and felt cannot rightly know," thought Mangus Colorado, but no words were expected of him by any of his people.

"All would have been well," said Shi-ka-she, "had they not fired the wagons at us."

No words were required for that. Shi-ka-she did not expect words. In the lofty fastness of his stronghold, sitting by the pallet of his elder brother, who had been close to death for many days, Shi-ka-she was reaching conclusions which the other had reached long before:

"When we have bows and arrows, they have the firesticks. When we have fire-sticks, they have the powder and ball in one piece. When we secure them, they bring others that shoot twice as far, then still others that shoot many times without reloading. Then they mount their guns on wagons, and a score of our people fall when the sound shakes the mountains—"

The voice of Shi-ka-she rose and fell. This was his song of lament, voicing the cry of all his people—

"Where we go only to the ends of our borders, they pass through all borders. Where we go forth in tens, they come in thousands. When we would have an end of war, they have not begun. Though we make friends with one, another destroys the friendship. There is no end to the Meh-hi-kanos, they are never still. The days of our people are numbered."

To all of which there was no need of answer, for these things had been thought of long since, and brooded upon in silence over many fires. . . . But that all men should be suddenly carried forward in a single great purpose to save the life of one, accomplishing things that would not be attempted except under great emergency—this had not yet been sufficiently pondered—

Nor the one secret thing above that: Not in the flesh, the Padre returning, but in a dream so clear that word by word was remembered. . . . "Even so, my brother, we shall meet again—"

This was substance of pondering without end.

LXV

H E LAY in the sun and shade, keeping his secret well. At night when all but the watchers slept, he sat alone by his small windy fires. They brought him short fat pieces of lodge-pole that would burn long. All that one chief could give another Shi-ka-she gave, but Mangus Colorado longed for his own mountains even though winter was coming. He tried his feet upon the ground, but laid them out to rest again. There was little breath to spare—

He healed very slowly; far more rapid and revolutionary was the change that took place in his understanding. Now he well knew that it would have been far better if Shi-ka-she had listened to Beela-chezzi; even acceded to the demands of the tonto teniente pending the coming of a wiser man; also he knew there was no future whatsoever for their people in a continuance of war against the Meh-hi-kanos. On any terms he wanted the long-time peace. . . .

Many miners were at work in the Pinos Altos and a portion of the great army that had passed through the Chihuicahuis occupied the mountains of the Mimbrenos to the north. According to his word Shi-ka-she announced his readiness for joint campaign against these, but Mangus Colorado said:

"I myself will go first and see."

It was not his way to tell others what was in his mind, but to act, then to let others speak. He took the hand of Shi-ka-she and lifted it to the place of the wound. A last time he crossed the grass, smelling the dust of the Baked Lands in the night, traveling very slowly. At the

267

Warm Springs he rested, his own people about him, a restless whispering people. His own establishment gathered close about him, women he had not known for long and many children whose time he had forgotten, and the exact person of their mothers.

He regarded them closely and asked no questions. This he knew among the great changes in his understanding —that those of his own blood were not set apart from others in his eyes as aforetime, that all were his people. But he did not confuse them with such thoughts, which were of the strangeness of old men who dream unduly. Even the days were chill; the sun far to the south tarrying very briefly on the slopes, except in the open places among the mountains.

One day his warriors brought in a Nakai-yi who had shown himself under a white cloth. Mangus Colorado was wanted by the white nan-tan of the Meh-hi-kanos now camped in the mountains to the north, this Nakai-yi said. If Mangus Colorado would come of his own accord, presents would be given and a covenant made. If he refused to come soldiers would be sent for him. They would hunt him out until he was found. One party of Meh-hi-kanos had already been sent out to look for Mangus Colorado—

The Mimbrenos took counsel together. Geronimo said:

"This Nakai-yi is not to be trusted. The Meh-hi-kanos are not to be trusted in sending a Nakai-yi—"

The messenger was questioned as to whether he came from the main body of soldiers, or from the smaller party already looking for Mangus Colorado.

The Mexican answered that he came from the smaller

party of Captain Shi-lan-de,* now waiting near the camp of the miners in the Pinos Altos.

"I myself would not go," said Geronimo. "This is but a trick to take our war lord captive. We have not numbers to drive out the Meh-hi-kano soldiers, even with the help of the Chihuicahuis, but the Meh-hi-kanos are never still. We can hide from them until they pass about their own wars. We will then drive out the rock-scratchers and have our lands again."

But Mangus Colorado had already decided. This was better than he had hoped, for it was in accord with his own will, to seek the nan-tan of the Meh-hi-kanos alone, even if he had not been sent for to receive presents and make a covenant. The messenger was released to say to El Capitan Shi-lan-de that Mangus Colorado was coming. The words of Geronimo were not accepted, for the Mimbrenos believed the decision of their war-lord invincible. Many would have gone with him, but Mangus Colorado forbade all but a few young men of his own teepees. Geronimo had no thought to go.

Soon afterward Mangus Colorado looked down the long open slope of the miners from the level timbered place where the ninyas had combed their hair. Then he passed on to the northward, making no great effort toward concealment. Among the peaks of the Pinos Altos, on an open shoulder, where nothing grew on account of the sweep of the winds, he halted at high noon. Presently a hail sounded from ahead and below. Mangus Colorado stood forth and raised his right hand.

---

*Captain Shirland, California Volunteers.

A figure appeared from the thicket, and this was no soldier, neither in blue nor gray coat, but one in the garb of the rock-scratchers.

"Others are behind him of his own kind," whispered the Apaches.

Mangus Colorado had already seen these. He called in Spanish for the leader to approach. In answer he was told to come forward part way. This he did, beckoning his followers to retire behind the rim of the hill. The two men came together. Though the solitary Meh-hi-kano* was a tall man, he came but to the shoulders of Mangus Colorado. Spanish greeting was exchanged. The white man touched the shoulder of Mangus Colorado and turned to his men. There was a stirring in the thicket, a movement of rifles not to be missed.

"To make talk with the nan-tan of the Meh-hi-kano soldiers—I come," said Mangus Colorado who knew now he was covered.

"I will take you to him. Come with me. Your followers will not be wanted."

The figure of Mangus Colorado straightened. For a space of seconds he considered, then turned to those behind him. "Tell my people to look for me when they see me," he said in Spanish and followed down the slope.

The Meh-hi-kanos were about him, laughing, slapping their leader on the shoulder.

"For talk with the soldier nan-tan, I myself come," said Mangus Colorado.

The answer from the leader was for Mangus Colorado

---

*Jack Swilling of the Walker Party, looking for gold in the Pinos Altos at this time.

to keep his shirt on, the force of which was not clear, since he had no thought otherwise. Laughing and talking, they continued down the slope until blue coats were seen waiting and one with shoulder-mark—addressed "Captain Shi-lan-de"—came quickly forward.

This was no great nan-tan of the Meh-hi-kanos, but another boy-man in leadership.

LXVI

Mangus Colorado was very tired. He plucked a handful of nettles and raised his arm to halt. Sitting upon a rock, he briskly spanked his knees and thighs with the prickly branches. His breathing was audible and he pointed to his chest. One said in Spanish:

"Pretty sick—it will soon be over."

All laughed at that.

The winter sun was low when he reached the hills from which the white teepees of the soldiers could be seen.

"Big nan-tan of the Meh-hi-kanos?" Mangus Colorado asked.

"Muy grande—" said El Capitan.

This hope alone remained: that after all foolish laughter, the nan-tan yet to be seen would prove the one whom he had so long sought. Great nan-tans of the Meh-hi-kanos were difficult to understand. Nan-tan Kah-han-hee had not wanted war, but mules; Nan-tan Four Eyes had spoken much of peace but had lacked justice, withal his setting of boundaries. Some nan-tans were very brave. Perhaps this one would be like Keet Kah-sohn in whom Shi-ka-she could find no fault whatsoever.

The Meh-hi-kanos were taking down their flag. A soldier made his evening song from the brass throat. The Great Nan-tan came to meet him.* He made laughing talk with Shi-lan-de Capitan. Now he stood before Mangus Colorado. The hair of his face was of two colors and the laugh under the hair boded no good. One stood by

---

*Colonel J. R. West, of the California Volunteers.

to make Spanish of his words. Another to put down in writing what was said.

". . . Long time we look for you, Mangus Colorado—"

"When word come for me, I myself come."

"And what do you now expect?"

"To make long-time peace between Meh-hi-kanos and my people, I come—"

"Very late in the day," laughed the nan-tan.

"Indian rest for this day. Mañana make peace talk."

"So you think you're here for talk, Mangus Colorado?"

"To make the long-time peace—"

"We know a better way than talk for that."

"My people do as I myself say—"

"Sure they do. In all the country of the Southwest, you are the worst Indian—"

"My people—no bad people—"

"You have made more trouble than any other Indian. We have followed your trail for five hundred miles by burnt bodies and cut throats. This time you have come to the end of your rope. Tomorrow morning we will see to that—tonight, if you make the slightest move to escape—"

He made imperative gestures to his men, which Mangus Colorado understood. The interpreter spoke a last time: "The slightest move to escape and you will be shot down, Mangus Colorado."

"No try to escape. I come to make long peace. Of my own will, I alone come—"

Thus Mangus Colorado saw the web close. It was very cold. The fire was plenty big but in an evil place. His blanket was thin. A sentry stood near with a long knife on his gun. Others walked up and down, their figures lost in the dark and returning. They laughed at the great body huddled back of its high knees. A Nakai-yi from the cook fires came close for a long look.

"His leg bones are like the shank of a mule—his head would fill a great cask," the Nakai-yi said.

A soldier poked the fire. His rod slipped—the sparks flying over the prisoner. Mangus Colorado brushed the clinging cinders from his blanket.

"I am not a child to be played with," he said looking around for an officer. He knew enough to despise enlisted men, who had to stand still and bring their hands to their heads when a nan-tan passed. There was no nan-tan in sight. One of the sentries laughed; another was heating his bayonet in the windy fire. He lifted the point often to look. The tip was faintly red. Mangus Colorado did not let him see he was watching.

The light still burned at the core of his brain. He was very still. His time had come. The Medicine Padre had seen far and seen true. The days of his people were numbered. The bridge was broken—

A sudden searing burn touched the base of his spine. He veered about but did not rise. He saw the sentry's rifle come to his shoulder. Now he knew. They were trying to goad him into attempting escape.

No nan-tan was in sight. He would not raise his voice to call aloud.

Another soldier poked the fire. This time a brand fell across his knees. He leaped up. That drew the shots upon him, even from outside the circle of firelight.

THE END.